# How I Became A Living Testimony

# By

# Byron Conway

# Acknowledgments

First of all, I would like to give praise and glory to the one, the almighty one who chosen me, created me, protected me, and guided me, the Lord our God. There's so many people that I would like to thank. One being the real mother that they left my side, my grandmother Hazel Flowers. I would like to thank my aunts, Beatrice, Brenda, Anna, Charlene, Verna Mae, Maxine, Roxan. My uncles John Dale, Jerry, and Leroy. My sister, Sheneka Bryant. My ex-wife Laquisha and her family, Rick, Brenda, Wallace, Wyquita, and Montrael. Also special thanks goes to my friend Robert Anderson. And a host of many more. James Larry Ashley, Chaplin Don Yancey, Joe Page III, Chris Budnik, Jess Spence, Shakara Green, Kathina Harper, Marcus Brawley, Cedric Anderson, Keya Brooks, John Earl, Donna Bost, Deani Smith, Jason Sanders, Travion Lee, Harold Allen, Steven Williams, Chilton Blunt, Timothy Ridley, Sheryl Orr, Bryant N Paulin, Casey Marlow, Darrell Scroggins, Rodney Dinwiddie, Eric Gaines, Roni Bowman.

# Rest In Love

Kimberly Stewart
Havannia Trotter-Flowers

## Rest In Peace

Lucy Burns
Lucille Thomas
James Flowers
Louise Murphy
Nolan J. Flowers
Johnny B. Flowers
Ruthie Dotson
Ivory Conway
Tomeka Hayes
William Hayes
Jacqueline Stewart
Bennie Stuart
Willie Conway
Leroy Flowers
Joe L. Flowers
Rita Flowers
Ola M. Kyles
Pam Scroggins
Helen Anderson
Ali Thomas
Flora L. Sumler
Albert Palmer
Larry Hill
Nicky Hill

Gregory Sharp
Janette Swift
Walter Swift, SR.
Gloria Gillard
Theresa Gillard
Velma Smith
James McDonald
William E. Johnson
Dr. Max Odom
Jean Scott
James Black
Marlon Marshall
Mickey Snell
Burn Daniels
Rhonda Brooks
John H. Stuart
Michael Witherspoon

# Foreword

Tests. Everyone has them. But not everyone passes them or gathers the discipline needed to help them grow and mature. Consequently, we are left with bitterness, hate, and unforgiveness that cripple us and leave us in a place of blaming others for what we go through. We allow the pain and hurt from such trials to distract us from their purposes. And with no regard to seek for understanding, we rather blame God for our painful experiences as if He had dealt us a bad hand. However, there are many who have gone before us and have experienced painful and life-threatening tests which allowed them to rely on the grace of God and cling to hope for better future. These are biblical authors, who have left us with the keys to enduring tests and trials. Among these authors, James reveals to us, both the purpose of tests and trials and what our response to those tests and trials should be. In James, chapter one, verse two, we are instructed to "Count It All Joy" when we face various trials. In verse 3, we are given the purpose of tests which are to develop patience. Ultimately, the one who understands the purpose of tests and chooses to respond in a manner of faith, is one who will complete, mature, finished, and lacking nothing (verse 4). That's right! Our response should be a "Faith Response." Though it doesn't feel good to us, by faith we know that it is good for us. Note Romans 8:28 which says, "And we know that all things work together for good to them that love God, to them who are called according to his purpose." There is indeed a purpose for your tests. And that purpose, my friend, may involve you, but it's much bigger than you. There are others who may experience the thing you are experiencing now, and in order to show them how to get through it, you must first endure! Books, I have learned, can teach a man many things. But experience can be one's greatest teacher. In his book, "How I Became A Living Testimony" Byron Conway shares the pains from his troubling past and the consequences he has had to face as a result of not responding correctly to them. It's obvious that his journey toward healing, restoration, and deliverance hasn't been an easy one. But as he reveals the obstacles he had to overcome in order to experience the love, joy, and peace of God during his most trying times, may you be inspired and empowered to do the same. Your test wasn't created for your demise, but was created for discipline and development. As spoken in the powerful lyrics of Gospel recording artists, The Selvy's, "If you go through your tests...knowing that God knows what's best...in the end you'll see...you'll have a testimony..."


-Arnold Lamont Parks, JR
Author of "Chronicles of A Warrior: A Journey To Complete Freedom."
Scripture verses used are from the King James

Saved

# 1
# The Nightmare Begins

There's a malevolent, evil force in our world to be sure. You see, I've experienced it firsthand...those temptations and snares that Satan used to do us harm. And yes, there are always those that will shun the idea of an "Evil One." But I'm here to recount the horrors that Satan and his minions have unleashed on my life. In fact, were it not for God's grace and mercy, I surely would not have survived these attacks. So, come along with me as I recount God's glorious love, meant for all of us, that led me on is merciful path to redemption and new life.

> *"Eye hath not seen nor ear heard, neither have entered into the heart of man, the things which God hath prepared for them that love him."*    1 Corinthians 2:9

At twelve years old, I didn't know who the Lord, Satan, or who Job was. Nor did I know who was I to blame for the physical pain and emotional distress that my sister and I were experiencing. Satan went from going to and fro in the earth, and from walking up and down in it, to walking into my family's home. He was here. In my home, in my mind and in my soul. He was here carrying out his orders...to take me out.

"Aaaahhhh," I cried in torment.

"Shut up and be still." My mother yelled at me.

"It hurt," I cried out to her. The pain was unbearable. Inexplicable. "When was the torture going to end?" I asked myself. I could see the hatred in Satan's soldier's eyes as he swung the extension cord back and forth across my bare skin. Who deserves such torture at the age of twelve? This wasn't the first time Satan's soldier, my step father, had brutally beaten me in front of an audience – my mother. Who else could help me? God? Who was that? My mother never mentioned him.

"Get your butt up and go get in the damn tub," my mother barked at me. She grabbed me by the arm and pulled me into the bathroom. She basically pushed me into the hot water.

"Ahh, momma, it's hot." I told her trying to get out the water.

"You better not," she threatened, raising her hand to hit me. I stood in the water crying and trembling. The stinging hot water felt like razor blades being dragged back and forth across my skin. The bruised welts on my body had swollen. I just stared at my mother as she walked out of the bathroom and closed the door behind her. Seconds later, I heard my sister screaming. I wanted to help her, protect her, but right now I can't even protect myself. I couldn't believe that we were beaten for something so small...just leaving soap suds in the sink after we washed dishes. Or for leaving the dishes in the dish rack and not drying them.

Tary was my sister's biological father. I was exactly as he treated me as - a step-child. I could've understood the difference in relations, but what I couldn't understand was, how he could beat his own child. Tary was a coast to coast truck driver. Veneka and I were happier when he was gone than when he was home. Because when he came home, we already knew what time it was. All hell broke loose. Our mother, it seemed like always had a bag of dirt on us to give to Tary. To her, she enjoyed seeing her own kids get beaten or thrashed. It was entertainment to her.

I sat in the water. My body was compacted with pain. Not just the usual pain. This pain was different. My mind comprehended the hot water as cruel and unusual punishment. The one thing that was created to assist me in life and to nurture me, was now unwanted and causing me pain. I knew then that water was vice versa. I was scared. Not only for me, but for my sister also. We were helpless in a world of the unknown. We were innocent, deprived of a childhood that the average kids were given by their parents, biological or step. I sat in the bathtub with all these thoughts going through my head. Getting rid of them wasn't an option because they were real. Reality had made its presence known. And so did my mother.
"Get out the tub, boy," my mother said, standing in

the door of the bathroom. My sister was standing behind her, crying. I got out of the tub and grabbed the dry towel so that I could dry myself off. The ruffles of the towel dragged across the swollen welts on my body. My skin had become numb by now.

"Hurry up, boy," my mother rushed me as I pulled up my underwear. I walked out the bathroom door past my sister. She was still crying and shaking. I looked her over as I walked past her to make sure that she wasn't bleeding anywhere. I went and crawled under my sheets and blankets, making sure not to irritate the welts. Moments later, I heard my mother telling my sister to get out the tub. I laid in bed thinking about what was next for me and my sister. I finally became comfortable and fell asleep.

We were neglected by the very person who was supposed to care for us. Momma. Our mother had changed since Tary's arrival. Prior to this, our mother was a loving and caring mother. She did whatever she needed to do to provide for us. I remember days when I would look into the refrigerator to find only a box of baking soda, milk that had spoiled because there was no cereal and some leftover chili beans still in the pot that they were cooked in. I remember those days when I would see my mother escort a man to her room. Later, she would leave and return with car trunk full of groceries.

Satan's soldier was gone back on the road. My sister and I were back to normal. Free of fear. My sister and I became close after our sister Kim died of pneumonia. My younger brother, Edward, was placed in the custody of his father. Edward was gone. Kim, too. So, now all I had left to share my childhood with was Veneka.

We always made fun of Veneka, because she reminded you of Whoopi Goldberg. Black with a pretty smile. She, like me, had gotten used to the little southern town of Nashville, Arkansas.

Nashville was a small town, just above the four- thousand population mark. It was known for its Tyson Foods chicken processing plant. The only other job worth looking at was Poulan weed-eater. On Friday and Saturday nights, you normally heard of people around the neighborhood getting together to play the card game spades. Crack cocaine hadn't hit the town hard yet. So all the wanna be dough-boys rode around in their mc's and cutlass cars, sitting on five-star and hammer rims.

"Byron," my mother's voice flared through our Jim Walter home. "Have you taken that trash out to the street, so that trash man can pick it up?"

"Yes, ma'am," I responded. I knew if I would've said anything besides that, there would've been some consequences. Veneka and I didn't only respond to my mother in that fashion, but to other adults also. Respecting your elders was one thing that I can say that she taught us.

"Moshellia," my mother called out to my sister. We knew that our mother was serious when she called us by our middle name. We knew to show our faces right then.

"Ma'am," Veneka answered.

"Are you finished cleaning that living room?" our mother asked.

"Yes, ma'am," Veneka responded, looking like a young aunt Jamima, wearing a black bandanna around her head to keep her hair intact for school.

Veneka and I didn't mind going to school. We loved anything that made us have to be away from home. We loved our home. Just not the people who ruled the home. We had the same things as the other low-income families. Everything we had from refrigerator to furniture was from the local rent to own store and our clothes came from the normal place as they always did, Wal-Mart.

Here we were again, in pain together. I stared at my step-father as he swung the thick leather belt across my sister's bare legs. This was another form of entertainment for my mother and step-father. My sister was losing the strength in her arms. The stack of encyclopedias was too much for her to hold up. We stood side-by-side in our underwear, holding stacks of encyclopedias in our hands, palms up and arms stretched out.

"Get' em up," Tary would holler at my sister, with the belt drawn back and ready to strike.

"I can't," Veneka would tell her father as she cried and trembled in agony.

"You better..." Tary threatened, clenching his teeth. Veneka would lift the books, because she knew what the next action was going to be. A lashing. Our mother just sat there. What had Tary done to her? She never showed any sympathy for us. It's like she didn't have a heart or soul anymore. She would just sit there like she no longer possessed any authority over her own children.

"Boy, get them damn books up," Tary growled at me. The encyclopedias would start getting the best of me after about an hour. I was a soldier. I had gotten used to the pain now. I always knew that it would come to an end in a couple of hours.

Afterwards, Veneka and I would release from the strongholds of Satan's soldier and we would take our baths and go to our separate rooms.

"Y'all better get 'em up," Tary roared at us. I was never worried about me. My baby sister was my focus. At this time is when the "I wish" thoughts came to mind. "I wish my daddy was here." I thought to myself. I knew a little about my father, David, even though he lived only minutes from me. All I heard about him was he knew how to use a shotgun and that's what he was known for, shooting people. I was his only child and I knew how protective he was of me. I knew this more than anything. If he knew what Tary was doing to me, not just me, but my sister too, he would kill Tary on the spot. No questions asked.

The nightmare was over once again. Tary was gone back on the road. But little did he know...

*"Whose shall offend one of these little ones which believe in me, it were better for him that a millstone were hanged about his neck, and that he were drowned in the depth of the sea."* Matthew 18:6 K.J.V.

# 2
# GONE

Things had become worse over time. The torture now was the "usual" to me and Veneka. We just went with it until we began to run away from home. We even came up with a plan to disclose to the police that Tary sold marijuana. That didn't work. I wondered why my sister continued to run away from home. There was some abuse allegations secretly discussed between the adults in our family. I would, at times, trying to tune in and ear hustle some info. But to no avail. It wasn't until my sister was sent off to a girl's home that I found out what had happened. My sister told my mother that her father was abusing her another kind of way. My mother didn't believe her own baby girl. She sent my sister away from me. I was sad. My sister was my heart.

I was the man of the house while Tary was on the road. I had to take on adulthood at an early age. I was given the responsibility of a father or husband a few years before. I had to take care of my siblings while my mother went clubbing or out with her friends to play cards. I had to pay my sister, Kim, the most attention because she was paralyzed from the neck down. She suffered from a spinal meningitis health condition. Meningitis was a condition that consisted of inflammation of the meninges usually caused by a bacterium or virus and characterized by fever, vomiting, intense headache and stiff neck. I had to feed Kim through a tube that was connected to her stomach. It didn't matter what I had to do. I did it because I knew that they depended on me. Now, it was only me and Veneka.

The day had finally come. We were on our way to pick up my sister. I was excited. We pulled up in front of the building. The sign out front read "Step n Stones." My mother got out of the car and went inside. I waited patiently in the backseat. Minutes later, my mother came out with Veneka behind her. Veneka got in the backseat with me. We hugged each other.
"How was Tary getting away with so much bad stuff?" I wondered. I didn't know, but someone mightier than Tary did.

*"Behold ye among the heathen, and regard, and wonder marvelously for I will work a work in your days, which ye will not believe, though it be told to you"* -Habakkuk 1:5 K.J.V.

I didn't understand what we were going through. I wasn't big enough to fight him nor did I have a gun. It was a good thing that I didn't, because my footsteps would've been the same as my father. Veneka was back at home. I was worried about her. I should have known something was going on. Tary had come home from a road trip. My mother was gone. Tary sent me to the store to get a loaf of bread. I returned home and knocked on the door. I knocked a few more times. Then I went around the house looking through the windows. I went back to the front door. Finally, Tary opened the door. I walked into the kitchen and put the loaf of bread on the table. Veneka was standing at the cook stove, stirring a pot and crying. I looked at Tary. I knew then that something was wrong. I wanted to know, but I was left with no answers. Tary went back on the road. We continued on with our normal lives. Once again, it was my sister and I. And oh, mother mayhem. My sister, Veneka, was my shadow; rain, sleet, or snow. Whenever you saw me, you saw her also. I don't know about other brothers, but I would fight a whole busload of kids about my sister. If she fought, I fought with her. No questions asked, whether she was right or wrong.

Living as a kid in Nashville, I had the opportunity to see the totally opposite brother-sister relationship. I personally saw brothers leave their sisters to fend for themselves. But not me. That just goes to show you how people's lives are different. We look at the situation from our own perspective; interpret it into what we think it is. However, we would never have thought that there was a reason behind it.

In the Bible, Joseph's brother did him the same way. Why? Because of hate, envy, and jealousy.

*"Come now therefore, and let us slay him and cast him into some pit, and we will say, some evil beast hath devoured him: and we shall see what will become of his dreams."* - Genesis 37:20 K.J.V.

The hell-bound works of the flesh were the primary reasons why brothers and sisters warred with each other. One factor for this was a momma's boy or a daddy's girl who had likely experienced hardships of being left out.

Veneka was Tary's daughter, but I was his boy so-to-speak. He spent more time with me than he did with his own daughter. But when it became abuse time, I received the harshest punishment.

I knew that the next episode was coming. I had gotten into some trouble at school. When I got back home and faced him, I could see the rage in his eyes. His muscles were tense. The veins appeared in his arms as if they were going to blow.

"Boy, what did I tell you?" Tary yelled at me. He started beating me with a thick leather belt he kept for that purpose. I was trying to make sure that all the pain wouldn't land in the same spot. That's the technique that I'd learned watching a boxing match. I cried hysterically. I felt helpless again. Where was my mother? I asked myself, looking for her to intercede. I looked up. There she was standing in the doorway. Why was I looking for her? Reality set in. This beating didn't last that long. I rolled over and looked at him. His eyes were filled with wrath.

"Get in trouble at that damn school again and see what happens." He said. I wore some shorts that day. The welts and bruises were already changing color—darkening under my skin Friday came around. My mother had earlier promised me that I could go stay the weekend with my father. I was ready. My father lived twenty minutes from me.

Even though he was so close to me. I probably saw him ten times or less during my first eighteen years of life and I enjoyed every second of it. He was my hero. I heard many stories about my father. Some from my grandmother. Some from my mother and a few from him personally. My grandmother told me that when my mother was pregnant with me, my father used to come home drunk. He would take his shotgun and shoot at my mother. One time, my father's best friend had to push my mother out the way of a bullet that blew a hole in the couch. My mother told me that my father used to take her outside, stand her up beside a tree and shoot at her with his shotgun. My father always told me stories about the things my mother did. He told me that he came home one day and found me on the sofa crying. My mother was nowhere to be found. He rushed me to the hospital. My body temperature was so high that the nurse immediately stuck me in a tub of ice. My father told the nurse to take care of me. He left the hospital on a hunt. Not his favorite hunting, but a bad one. He went home and retrieved his 12-gauge shotgun. He went and picked up his best friend to take the ride with him. He already knew where my mother was—the small town of Bradley. A small town in southwest Arkansas. He stopped by the sheriff's office and told him what he was about to do. He asked around the town and found out where the man that my mother was with lived. This man was Tary.

My father pulled up to the home and got out the car as if he lived there. Standing with his shotgun in his arms, he called out my mother's name. "Callie Mae, I know you are in there. Come on so we can go home." My father said while scanning the house. He stood there for a few minutes. Finally he saw someone look through the curtains. "I know you're in there, Callie Mae. Come on now so we can go get Bryan out the hospital." he said, adding me to the equation. Someone looked through the curtain again. My father ran out of patience. He unloaded the shotgun in the exterior of the house. Whoever was in there ran out the back door. My father drove back to the hospital in Hope where he left me in the care of a nurse. When he made it back. I was in someone else's care; the Department of Human Services. DHS put me in a foster home.

In fact, I remember a weekend when I was 15 years old and spent the time of my life hunting with him and feeding his animals. My father may not have taught me as many things as other kids' fathers taught them, but he taught me one of the most important ones. He taught me about animals.

I didn't mention the abuse of my stepfather to my father. I didn't want to stir up strife. I wanted to enjoy our time together. Sunday came around. It was time for me to go home. My mother was smart. She sent me to my father's with pairs of blue jean pants. Even though it was summertime. My father and stepmother had bought me a new shirt and pair of shorts. My stepmother handed it to me and told me to go change. I excitedly went into the bathroom eager to try them on I looked at my legs. The welts had started to scab over. I sat on the toilet ashamed; not wanting my father to see what his son had suffered. After so long he came in. I looked down at my legs. He did the same. He looked at me.

"Son, what happened to you?" My father asked.
"Tary whipped me with a belt." I replied.
"He whipped you for what?" My father asked, looking at my legs.
"Because I got into trouble at school." I told him.
"Get your stuff," My father told me, walking out the bathroom door. I knew that something was about to happen. I just didn't know what. He called my mother and told her that his truck couldn't make it to Nashville and that he needed her to come pick me up. My mother knew that Tary was up the road and instead she told my father to take me up to the gym where Tary was playing basketball.

My father loaded us and his guns into his truck. I thought to myself that if my mother would've come there, she probably would have died that day. My father would've killed her. My father drove us to the gym.
"Get out and come with me, son." My father directed me. I got out of the truck and walked step-by-step with him. We entered the foyer of the gym and my father asked for Tary. Soon, Tary walked up in front of us.
"You have been beating on my son?" My father asked Tary.
"If the lil bastard is going to be staying under my roof..." that's all I heard Tary say.
Pow, pow, pow.
My father was shedding the shells out of his 22

pistol into Tary's flesh.

"Nooooo, daddy," I screamed running backwards. I ran out the gym. People were jumping fences trying to escape the gunfire. Car tires were screeching, horns blowing. I ran nonstop all the way up to my Aunt Charlene's house crying all the way. My cousin Aaron ran the opposite direction to my other aunt's house.

I only learned later the full details of the shooting. I found out that Tary took off running, being trailed by my father. Tary ran in a corner behind a gas stove and collapsed. My father emptied the pistol and walked out the gym. He got his shotgun out the truck and shot at the police officer responding to the shooting. Tary's friend put him in his car and rushed him to the hospital. The doctor told him that he would've dies if he hadn't have been so muscular built.

Tary got out of the hospital days later. He sat on the couch all bandaged up. He couldn't even look me in the face. It took him weeks to heal. Tary went back on the road. One day, my mother received a collect call from him. He was in jail in another state. He had been accused of rape. Veneka and I knew that the nightmare was over. Tary was.....Gone.

# 3
# Satan's Conspiracy Revealed

Perhaps the most shocking revelations in my young life came when I was 19 years old and employed at a chicken processing plant known as Tyson Foods in Nashville, Arkansas.

Tyson Foods, a family-owned company based in Springdale, Arkansas, was my second job since being released from prison. I had served 13 months for residential burglary. The chicken processing plant was a whole nother world to me. It gave not only me, but many of my family members a great opportunity to build on.

I had been out of prison for about eight to nine month. My life was finally back on track. I had a position in the debone department. I was a young workhorse. I did it all from cutting legs and shoulders to deboning thighs. I worked around females a lot. I was in my third or fourth relationship. That was another thing that I loved about the plant. It had relationship opportunities. There were more women than men. My sister, Veneka, also worked at the plant. I worked the second shift from 5pm to 2am, and she worked the graveyard shift from 12am to 6am. Because of the 2 hour overlap, my sister's sanitation crew would have to wait until my shift stop due to us working in the same pat of the plant. Veneka and I paths often crossed. When I would be walking out of the plant, she would be walking in. There's one night that I regretted that our paths crossed this particular night would change my life forever.

Veneka walked up to me. She had an enraged look on her face. She just started talking about issues that she had had with our mother. She just continued on and on. I allowed her to vent until she said something that caught my attention. "What did you say?" I asked her. She looked away from me. I asked her again to get clarification of what I thought she said.
"What did you say, Veneka?" I asked her again. She finally turned back towards me, "Momma tried to have you killed for some insurance money." She said, looking into my eyes with an "I'm sorry" look on her face. The words felt like someone had taken a fillet knife, sliced me across my brain and left a mental scar. She stood there and told me the whole story.

My mother had purchased a life insurance

policy. My best friend, who was Lacy at the time, was basically hired to lure me out into the woods, put two bullets in my head and leave me for dead. I thought back to the year of 1997. Three years earlier. My sister's story had some credibility to it. My friend did disappear all of a sudden around that time. He hadn't been seen since. I stood there, legs frozen and unable to move. I was in a terrible state of shock. My world had been shattered to pieces.

Tears began to roll down my face. I couldn't even catch them with my hand because pain wasn't meant to be caught with the hand but with comfort. Veneka looked at me, the tears and the pain. I could tell that she didn't know what else to say nor do. I walked away, crying. I took of waking down the street wondering, "Why?" Cars leaving the parking lot rolled past me, anxious to get to their destinations. I almost got struck by a speeding car. All types of things were going through my mind. The very one was the fact that my sister knew about this for three years and didn't tell me. My family had deliberately kept a secret from me. The pain hurt so bad until my head began to throb. My throat began to hurt. I clinched my fist and asked again, "Why?" I was so overwhelmed until when I came to; I was way out on the highway headed towards Hope, Arkansas. I told myself that I needed to go home before I got killed by a car. I turned around. It dawned on my where home was. Just so happen. I was living with my mother at the time. I had nowhere else to go. So I had to go back there.

I made it home. I put my key in the lock and unlocked the door. I stepped inside the living room and sat on the couch, not bothering to turn on the lights. I sat in pitch black darkness, crying, thinking that the woman that carried me for nine months and tried to take my life was only a few feet down the hallway asleep. I cried myself to sleep.

The revealing of Satan's conspiracy would then initiate a spiraling pattern of events. The first one came a few days later and would cost me my job.

One day I went to work. Females ran up to me. My friend, Lanice, did all the talking.
"You need to go check on your aunt." she told me pushing me towards the door.
"Where is she? What's wrong with her?" I asked Lanice.
"She's at your mother's house." she told me. I had moved out of my mother's house. I hadn't been there in some weeks I walked out of the plant and took off across the parking lot in a jogging-stride. Of all my aunts at that time, she still is my favorite aunt. Each one of them had their own special qualities. My aunt, Tanna, was the wisest one to me. She would be the one to always give me words of encouragement when it came to things

involving my mother. She was my heart. I made it to my mother's house in about ten minutes. My mother lived in a Jim Walter home that sat off the street in the center of the block.

I ran across the yard that used to be my basketball arena. I jumped up on the porch and opened the door. There she was drooped over on the sofa covered in blood. I stood there looking at her and gritting my teeth. My blood started to boil. She didn't have to tell me who the assaulter was. I already knew. It was her fiancé. He worked with me. He was going to pay for this. I turned around and ran out the door. My aunt started calling my name. She knew me. She knew what I had in mind. Satan did also, because he had control of it.

I ran full speed back to the plant. I put my smock and apron on and went to the debone line. My supervisor put me on the line beside Lanice. My aunt's fiancé worked only a couple of lines away from me. I stared at him with hatred in my eyes. He knew that I was furious and he knew why. I could hear Lanice talking to me. I knew that she was worried about me. I didn't have any understanding at the time. Lanice was attached to me. One time she heard me singing Lenny Williams song "I love you." After that, she asked for me to sing it to her at the least twice a week.

I could no longer hold back the rage that was

manifesting inside of me. For the second time at the plant, tears rolled down my face. People began to notice. Lanice patted me on my back and told me that it was going to be okay. No, it wasn't.

I walked off the line, knife in hand. I walked over to my aunt's fiancé and pointed the knife directly at his throat.
"If you ever put your hands on my aunt again, I will kill you. You understand?" I told him, making sure that he seen the tip of the knife. The plant supervisor ran out to the line where I was and grabbed me. They took me in the office. That was my last time seeing the inside of the plant. I was fired from my job. A few weeks later, I was back in jail for another burglary charge. I didn't know then, but God would reveal to me the same thing that he revealed to Jeremiah.

*"For I know the thoughts that I think toward you, saith the Lord, thoughts of peace, and not of evil, to give you and expected end."* -Jeremiah 29:11

When we experience bad things in life, the first thing we say is, "God, why did you do this?" Because of a lack of knowledge, we don't know that God doesn't cause the evilness that goes on in this world. Satan the Devil is the ruler here on Earth.

*"Let no man say when he is tempted. I am tempted of God: for God cannot be tempted with evil, neither he tempteth any man.*
*But every man is tempted, when he is drawn away of his own lust, and enticed. (For example: Hate and retaliation.)*
*Then when lust hath conceived it bringeth for sin: and sin (For example: Greed and Conspiracy), when it is finished, bringeth for death.* -
James 1: 13 - 15


We sometimes in life, heard people talk about Satan the Devil, but have never saw him. We've only seen images of what man has portrayed him to look like. Satan the Devil, also known as the adversary, is not of a physical form. So, he can't physically harm us. He uses deception. He deceives people. He also knew something that I wouldn't come to know and understand for over a decade. How powerful I was going to be.

# 4
# Please, Forgive Me

I was back in jail for the second time and on my way back to prison. I knew that I was guilty. So, I wasn't going to take a chance going to trial. I lay on my bed in my small cell, staring at the wall. This was the second time that I ended up in jail as a result of being a follower. But this is how leaders are formed. You remember the saying, "Everybody follows the leader."

There wasn't much to the living conditions. My cellmate and I had a small plug-in radio that stayed on the same station, that rested on a small steel table and had a steel stool connected to it. We took turns looking out the small square window that was covered with bars. We could see the parking lot. We would stand in the window for hours before and during visitation hours. I received an unwanted visit one day. God's promise and curse to man had struck my family once again.

"Byron, you have a special visit. Get dressed. I'll be back in a minute to get you," he said. I got myself together. I wondered who it was and why would they be coming during the week. The jailer had returned with the sheriff.

"Byron, your family is here to see you." the sheriff said. The jailer and sheriff escorted me to the booking room. Veneka, holding my three year old niece and my grandmother got up out of their seats and greeted me with a hug.

"Byron, we have some bad news," Veneka said. "What's wrong?" I asked, looking back and forth at the both of them.

"Momma died last night," my grandmother said. The news was devastating. I shook my head as I tried to comprehend the loss. My great grandmother was gone. I couldn't contain the hurt and pain.

"Naw, naw don't tell me that. She was all that I had. Y'all got to bring her back." I cried, as my sister hugged me. I looked at my grandmother. She was crying, not because her mother had died, but because she saw her grandson in pain and in confinement. This was the first time that I had ever seen my grandmother cry.

There's a reason why the loss of my great grandmother affected me so much. I never got the chance to say goodbye. I never got the chance to apologize to her for my mother's wrongdoing to her.

Some years ago, my mother, Veneka, and I often made trips to my great grandmother's house. "Y'all put some clothes on so we can go grocery shopping for your grandmother." Our mother would tell us. My great grandmother was my number one. She lived a couple hundred feet up the road from my grandmother. During the summertime, I used to walk up to her house to help her with her daily house and garden tasks. When I made it there, she would normally be bent over at the waist with a hoe in her hand, hoeing grass and humming an old church hymn.

"Let me get that, grandma." I would tell her, while taking the hoe out of her hand.

"Thank you, baby," she would respond, while smoothing out her old garden dress. "How's your grandmother doing down there?"

"She's doing okay."

Thing changed after that. I went from helping her to unknowingly stealing from her. That's what Satan did, though. He came to steal, kill, and destroy.

"Y'all find your granny's checkbook so we can go grocery shopping for her," my mother would tell Veneka and me before we got out of the car. We found the checkbook. We went grocery shopping. However, we never went back to great grandmother's house. We always went back home.

Veneka and I noticed the more we went back, the harder it was to find the checkbook. One day it all came out in the open. Our mother was writing checks and stealing my great grandmother's money out of the bank. That's what hurt me the most. I didn't get a chance to apologize.

For some reason, I didn't get to go to the funeral. Days past, I was awaiting transfer to prison. I had received my G.E.D. The first time that I was there. What would happen this time?

A female jailer came to the pod one day. She opened the door.
"Byron, come go with me," she said.  We walked to the other side of the jail. The jailer opened the food-flap on the door. I looked down. It was my mother. She had been arrested for a "Hot Check Violation." The jailer allowed us to talk for a minute. I could hear the Caucasian female inmates telling my mother that her son was cute. My mother was transferred to the women's unit at Newport, Arkansas. I soon was transferred back to the Varner Unit, also known as the "gladiator school." I was assigned to hoe squad. One day when we were turning out, a white truck pulled up beside my field rider. Next thing I know, my field rider called me over to the truck.
"You Byron Conway?" The man in the truck askcd.
"Yes sir," I responded, making sure to be

respectful.

"Alright,"

I went back and got in line with my squad. We walked side-by-side in a deuce to our work location. I looked up minutes later. The white truck was coming back. I noticed an Afro-American man on the back of the truck as it came across the field. The man looked familiar. I couldn't believe my eyes. It was my father.

It was 2001. My father had been in prison for five years for manslaughter. He killed his fiancé on a holiday. I would never forget the day.

On the fourth of July 1996, we sat at my grandmother's house watching television. We heard a car pull up in the yard. I looked out the door. It was my Aunt Mae. I knew something wasn't right because she never made that trip. She walked in the house.

"Hey y'all," she spoke.

"Hey Aunt Mae," I responded.

"Have you heard from your father this morning?" she asked.

"No ma'am. What's wrong?"

"He shot and killed Ruby this morning." She informed me.

"Oh my God," my grandmother said covering her mouth. My aunt let. I went to the jail to see my father. The nice sheriff allowed me to see my father. I was escorted to the visiting booth. I talked to him. That was the last time I saw him until now.

My father jumped off of the back of the truck.
"Hey daddy," I said.
"Hey son," he said, pulling me into his arms to hug me. The riders allowed us to talk for a while. My father and I hugged one last time. Then he got on the back of the truck. This would be the last time that I would see him until his release.
Sooner or later, I was transferred to the men's unit at Newport. The women's unit was right across the street. The men's unit was being run by a private company until the state took it over.

One day, I unexpectedly received a letter from my mother. She had sent a request to the wardens of both units and obtained permission to correspond with me.
I, in a way, was happy to hear from her even though she tried to have me killed. I opened the letter and began to reading it. My mother was apologizing to me all through the letter, but she never mentioned what she was apologizing for. But deep down in my heart, I knew what and why she was apologizing. Tis is one thing that the lord commanded us to do.

*"Confess your faults one to another, and pray for one another, that ye may be healed"* - James 5:16

# 5
# The Revealing Of Satan's Plan
# A

January 2002, I was released from prison. I paroled back to my mother's house again. I never knew why I went back there. She had been released from the women's prison a few months before I was released. My first night out, I had to spend the night at my uncle's house in Ashdown, Arkansas. A friend that I met at Newport had left his number with me before he left and told me to call him whenever I made it to Texarkana. I called him as soon as I got off the bus. His mother answered the phone. I asked her did she know where Will was at. She told me that she didn't know where he was. It was after midnight and I was slightly intoxicated. A friend that was released with me was from Texarkana. We had a four hour layover at the bus station in North Little Rock. So, while there, we took it upon ourselves to call a taxi. We had the taxi driver to take us to the nearest liquor store. We purchased a bottle of Paul Mason V.S.O.P. We went back to the bus station. A hustler sold us a bag of weed. My friend and I smoked the weed right there in the bathroom. Our bus arrived and we loaded the bus. We sat together, enjoying our freedom. The bottle was empty by the time we reached Hot Springs.

Now, I was at the bus station in Texarkana, not knowing who else to call this time of the night. Just when I was about to give up hope, Will came through the door. His hair was half braided.
"What's up bro? You ready?" he asked.
"Let's roll," I said.
"Check this out," he said, looking back at me as we walked to the car. "We have to make a stop first before we go home."
"That's cool," I said, getting in the car. We drove across town to where he had been getting his hair braided. We pulled up to some project apartments. We exited the car and went inside the apartment. He didn't bother to knock. He opened the door and went inside as if he lived there.
"Hey y'all, this is my homie Byron. He just got out of Newport where I was." He told the two women who were sitting in the living room.
"Hey," they greeted me in unison. They both looked to be in their 30s. One was a little heavier than the other. They both were decent looking. Will walked over and took his place back in the chair where he probably was sitting in when he

received my call. The smaller woman began to braid his hair.

"So, what you go to prison for?" the smaller woman asked me.

"Burglary," I told her. Being shy, I didn't say anything else. The three of them talked while I looked around my new environment. I could tell that they didn't live here alone or at all because the home had an elderly woman's setting. The subject about alcohol came up. The women wanted something to drink. Will didn't want to stop getting his hair braided. That left the younger female with the responsibility of traveling late at night to retrieve some liquor.

"Y'all know I don't know how to drive," she told the other two.

"B drive her to the store for me." Will said. Before I could protest, Will was tossing me the keys to his car. The female and I walked out to the car. Here I was, on my way to the liquor store. I hadn't been out of prison twenty-four hours yet and was already putting my freedom on the line. I drove the female to the liquor store. I felt odd driving another convicted felon's car with no driver's license, in another town, late at night to the liquor store. I made it to the liquor store and back safe and sound. The women drank their wine coolers, while Will and I passed up the opportunities. Will's braids were finished. It was time to go home. So, I thought.

"Bro, we can't go home just yet," he told me.

"What's up?" I asked him.

"I need to make a stop by this female's house."

"It's all good. I'm riding with you." I told him.

"This is the deal," he said. He explained the whole plan to me. I was going to drop him off at the female's house. Then I was going to take the car and drive back across town to the females' house that I recently had drove to the liquor store. Here I was again, back in the same situation. I found the address. I parked the car and walked up to the door. I noticed that I was in another set of projects. The projects were quiet. Not a single person was out. The door opened just as I was about to knock. It was her. The wine cooler drinker invited me inside. The place was dark. I followed her lead into the kitchen.

We sat down at the table across from each other. We chatted for a moment. Somehow, the conversation turned to music. We discovered that we had something in common. We both loved Gerald Levert's song "Answering Service."

"Oh, I love that song," she said, "I have that CD."

"I want to hear that song." I said.

"For real," she responded.

"Yes,"

I was already slow dancing in my chair. She got up and walked into the living room. Seconds later the song began playing. She came back in the kitchen and reached for my hands.

"Dance with me."

We danced to the song, grinding our pelvises together. She put her hands on my shoulders. I rested my hands on her hips. We slow danced like we were dancing to the last song being played in a Jamaican night club. One thing led to another. The next thing I knew, she was sitting in a chair with her legs upon my shoulders.

We said our goodbyes. I drove back across town to pick up will. It was really late when we made it to my uncle's house in Ashdown. He opened the door after I had knocked a few time. By it being late, we didn't talk much. The next morning, my uncle drove me to my mother's house in Nashville. She had been out a few months. She had already established a job working at a local gas station.

The second night that I was out, she had to go to work. Hours later, I walked to the gas station. I couldn't sleep. I had been up for two days. My mother was surprised when she saw me walk through the glass double doors.
"Boy, what are you doing out this time of night?" she asked me.
"I couldn't sleep." I told her as I looked around the store.
"Gone over there and sit down." she said, pointing at the lunch break tables. I went over and took a seat. I scanned the store back and forth, looking at

all of the goodies. Behind me was the fountain drink and Icee machine. To the right was the area were my mother stood, behind the counter with different brands of cigarettes hanging over her head. To her right was two separate shelves filled with candy bars, chips, and other items.

"You hungry?" my mother asked.

"Yes ma'am." I responded. My mother grilled me a big cheeseburger as customers came in and out of the store. My mother and I noticed something at the same time. A Caucasian female in her 20s kept coming in and out the store. The last time, my mother finally asked her.

"Girl, why do you keep coming in this store? Are you okay?" My mother asked the young woman. I was curious and wanted to know myself. The young woman was kind of cute. She stood about five feet and four inches tall and looked as if she weighed about 110 pounds. She had a smooth rounded face with shoulder length hair that was brown in color. She wore some blue jeans, a tee shirt, and some tennis shoes. She just stood there smiling at my mother with this "I'm innocent" look on her face.

The little light bulb must have clicked on in my mother's head.

"Oh, I know why," my mother said. Looking over at me, "Go ahead and take him with you."

I looked at my mother as if she had just given me away at a dating auction. The young Caucasian female came over to me, grabbed me by the hand and led me out the door. We got into her truck and left. I ended up with a stranger for the second night in a row.

Things didn't last long between my mother and me. After only a week or two, she was telling me that I needed to find me somewhere to stay. This wasn't the first time that my mother had put me out in the cold. She had been doing this ever since I was a teenager. It took me a long time to figure out why my mother hated me so much. I reminded her of someone every time she looked at me. My mother hated me because of my father.

When my mother was pregnant with me, my father physically and mentally abused her. He was an alcoholic. It was told to me that my father used to come home drunk. He would take my mother outside, stand her up beside a tree and shoot at her with a shotgun. Not only did she suffer from the trauma, but by her being pregnant with me. I would also end up suffering from the emotional effects.

My grandmother once told me this story. My father was drunk one night. He had his best friend at the house with him. He and my mother had a fallen out about something. My father went into the bedroom and retrieved his shotgun. He came out the room, pointed the gun at my mother and pulled the trigger. My father's best friend hurriedly pushed my mother out of the way. The shotgun blew a hole in the sofa. I still suffered the consequences of my father's actions.

The good Lord already had a place to stay reserved for me. My sister's grandmother took me in. I shared an add-on room with my sister's twin cousins, Erick and Derrick. One night, the twins and I were walking down the street. A white car pulled up beside us. The passenger window came down. It was some friends of ours. The next thing I noticed, the back passenger seat window came down. Someone called my name.

"Byron, is that you?" the backseat passenger asked.

"Yeah, it's me." I responded, trying to see who the passenger was. "Who is that?"

"It's me, Mesha," the passenger said.

"What's up, Mesha?"

"Nothing! What's up with you?" she asked eyeing me up and down.

"I'm just walking with Erick and Derrick. What's up with you?" I asked her.

"I'm just cruising with Robbie and Sonya." she said.

"That's what's up."

"Well, it was good seeing you again."

"You too," I said. They drove away.

Old memories began to come back. Mesha was

my childhood sweetheart. Her family and my family shared a place together. One morning, I got up early. I went and got in the bed with Mesha. She and my sister shared a bed together. I don't know if my sister was asleep or not. I didn't care. That wasn't going to stop me. I crawled on top of Mesha. She welcomed me. I had forgotten about everybody else in the house. I heard a voice behind me. An angry voice.

"Boy, I'm fixing to whoop your ass," My mother said. I already knew what time it was. I crawled out of the bed and went back into the living room. My mother came back through from the bathroom. She rolled her eyes at me. She returned seconds later with a belt and began to swinging it wildly at me. She didn't care where she hit me at. She was mad. While I was getting whipped by my mother, Mesha was getting whipped by her own mother. Then they traded. I knew that I had one more whipping to come. When my sister's father, Tary, returned home, he beat me like the step child that I was to him. I didn't know why then, but I would later find out the real reason.

Erick, Derrick and I walked around Nashville every night. One night, we didn't have a set destination. We just stood in the middle of the street looking at each other.

"Let's go up to Mesha's house," one of the twins said.

"Mesha," I quickly responded.

"Yeah, she doesn't live too far from here." Derrick said while pointing in the direction Mesha lived in. I was tired. I didn't want to go. I wanted to go home. They finally talked me into going. We made it to Mesha's apartment in only a few minutes. One of the twins knocked on the door. We could hear music playing inside. The door swung open. It was Sonya.

"Hey y'all. Hey Byron. What are y'all doing way up here?" Sonya asked us.

"We came to kick it with y'all." One of the twins told her.

"Come in," she invited us. The apartment was packed with people. Moments later, Mesha appeared out of nowhere. She smiled at me. Someone asked me to be their domino partner. I sat down at the domino table. I soon noticed that Mesha was standing behind me, watching me play. She smiled every time I won. It started to get late. The crowd began to thin out. I was standing with the twins getting ready to leave when Sonya walked up to me.

"Mesha wants you to stay after everybody leave." Sonya said, leaning towards my ear. I informed the twins on what was going on. They left. Everyone didn't leave. Mesha took me into a spare bedroom. We made love. Then we made it official. We were now a couple.

I had the same routine. I would wake up at my sister's grandmother's house, get myself together

and head for Mesha's house. I would return home before it got too late. One night, I made it home late. My step-grandmother was waiting on me. "Byron," she called out to me from her room. "Yes ma'am," I put my coat down and walked to her bedroom. I knocked on the door.
"Come in and have a seat, baby." she said. We both sat watching her television at first. Then she finally said something. She brought up a car wreck that I was in.

Back in 1997, my mother had this car. She pretended like something was wrong with the car. All of a sudden, she came up with this brilliant idea for the car to be wrecked and that I should be the one to do it. I was living with my mother at this time. I knew that if I didn't do it, she would put me out again. I would be homeless. I felt pressured. I finally agreed to do it. I found a place to wreck the car. The day had come. We stopped and got my uncle's car. My mother and sister trailed me. I reached the wreck location going over the speed limit. All kinds of things were going through my head. I was there now. There was no turning back. I drove off the road into a steep-grassy drop off.

The car rolled uncontrollably a few hundred feet and crashed into a tree. The airbag instantly imploded, hitting me hard in the face. I was dazed. My face had a stinging sensation coming from it. I came to. I tried to unlock the seat belt, but couldn't.

It was jammed. So, I maneuvered my way out of it. My mother and sister looked surprised when they see me crawling out the window out the car. They scrambled to get out of my uncle's car. I staggered – walking towards the road. When I passed by them, they looked at me like I was Houdini and had just finished performing a magic trick. I got in my uncle's parked car and pulled away. I went down the road and got some ice from my friend. He asked questions about what happened. I blew him off. They were just putting my mother and sister in an ambulance when I came back through. The auto body guy labeled my mother's car as totaled. Days later, I was homeless. For some apparent reason, she put me out anyway.

My sister's grandmother continued to talk about the car wreck. It was like she kept giving me hints. God finally instilled it in me. I burst out in tears. "Oh my God," I cried hysterically. "She wanted me to die in that car wreck."
"Yep," my sister's grandmother said. She explained the whole plan to me. My mother wanted me to die in that car wreck. She would've gotten a two-for-one. Not only the car insurance, but the life insurance also. I knew then why she and my sister looked surprised when they saw me crawling out of that car wreck. My mother thought evil against me just like Jacob thought evil against his own son Joseph. But God had something else in mind. This is what Joseph told his father;

*"Bu as for you, ye thought evil against me; but God meant it unto good, to bring it to pass, as it is this day, to save much people alive."* -Genesis 50:20

God had revealed to me Satan's Plan A. After his first plan failed, he implemented his Plan B. My friend Lacy, which also failed. There was not one, but two plots. I was still alive, but really didn't know how.

# 6
# The Happiest Day of My Life

"Welcome to adulthood." I thought to myself as I looked around the apartment Mesha and I shared together. She had asked me to move in with her only weeks after I was out of prison. To someone else, the apartment may have not seemed much to them but to Mesha and me, it was our own little castle. Our home occupied the usual interior decorative things that everyone else in the projects could afford. In the living room, the average three-piece furniture set could be seen as soon as you came through the front door. A small coffee table rested in front of the long sofa, surrounded by smaller square end tables with matching lamps. A Zennox television sat on top of an old wooden stand that was covered with a sheet. And the curtains were the normal flower design that the lower-class people purchased from the nearest dollar store. This was our home.

Things didn't go as I planned them in prison. While in prison, I wrote a motion picture screenplay, a mover. My intentions were to get out and sell it. Then, I didn't even know what a copyright was. That plan quickly failed. I somehow lost the script. I had to come up with a new plan. It was hard for me to maintain a steady job by me being fresh out of prison. Due to the hardships and continuing involvement of prison life, most men become affected in different ways. So that leaves them emotionally and mentally unprepared to hold a job. A convicted felon is labeled as a depressed minority. Basically, the government has declared that had you not had emotional problems, you would have been able to conform to the rules of society.

The government assistance I knew of then was food stamps. Mesha's mother, Linda, lived directly across from us. We spent majority of our time visiting her mother and her husband "Mick." They were good people and supportive of us. I got along with her brothers and sisters, especially, Nita. Nita lived with us. She was seventeen years old. She was always in and out with her friends. She was the youngest sister. I didn't talk to the other sister, Tesha, that much. She seemed to be antisocial. She didn't talk much. I still treated her like she was family. I was the closest to Mesha's two brothers, Trael and Bug. We often went on brother-in-laws ventures. If you saw me, I most likely would've been with one or the other, or both.

I recall my first birthday after my release. Trael and his girl and Mesh, took me to Texarkana for my twenty-third birthday. We went bowling. I remember Mesha tapping me on the shoulder and handing me a drink. I took the glass out of her hand and taking a swig, I almost spit it out.

"Mesha, what's this?" I asked her, grabbing my throat. She thought it was funny. She just stood there laughing at me. She grabbed me by the hand and led me to the bar.

"Show him what the drink was that you made for him." she told the bartender. The woman behind the counter grabbed the bottle with the red label and handed it to me.

"Bacardi Rum 151," I said while taking another light sip of the clear liquor. The Bacardi was good, but had a good kick to it also. I hadn't done too much drinking cause of the fact that I was still on parole. I wanted to stay on track so that I could do what I had in mind and also what Moses said in the book of Genesis.

*"Therefore shall a man leave his father and mother, and shall cleave unto his wife: and they shall be one flesh."* - Genesis 2:24

Mesha didn't have a clue as to what I had staged for her; the marriage proposal. I took it upon myself to do the traditional thing. I asked her family first. I asked the sisters and brothers also. They all were excited. I asked Mesha's step-father because her biological father lived forty-five minutes away. I waited until she had come in from work one day. I had the engagement ring ready that I had paid out through a local jewelry store's layaway plan. She came through the door. Nita and one of her friends came in behind Mesha, smiling. They already knew the plan.

"Hey bae," Mesha said, pecking me with a kiss on the cheek.

"Hey love," I responded by turning my other cheek so that she could kiss it also. I just looked at her and smiled. Nita and her friend smiled at each other.

"What's wrong with y'all?" Mesha asked.

I swallowed, then inhaled and exhaled. I stood up and pulled the ring out of my pocket. Mesha covered her mouth with her hand. I lowered myself down on one knee and popped the big question that I thought that I would never ask a woman.

"Mesha, will you marry me?" I asked, holding her hand.

"Ooh, Bae, Yes!" she said. I slid the ring on Mesha's finger. It was a size too big.

"Don't worry about that," she said, "we'll get it downsized."

Nita and her friend, Shelley, clapped their hands. Mesha pulled me up on my feet and we embraced in a deep kiss. We walked across the sidewalk to her mother's apartment and gave them the news. Mesha and I were anxious to get married. We set the date for July. First thing first, we purchased the invitations. Then we found someone to make the wedding cake. I allowed Mesha to pick the wedding colors and make the arrangements.

Once again, things didn't go as planned. I hadn't found a job and Mesha had quit her job. The wedding situation came up. Something about canceling the wedding.

"I'm not canceling my wedding." Mesha told her mother.

"Well, what are you going to do?"

"I don't know. I'll figure out something." Mesha said.

"Well, you better figure out something quick because you only have a few days." Mesha's mother told her.

I was in deep thought. Nothing had been paid for, but only the invitations which we had already passed out. My uncle J.D. was my best man. My brother, first cousins and my brother-in-laws were my groomsmen. Mesha had picked my sister and her sisters to be her matron-of-honor and bridesmaids. I knew that Mesha was expecting this day to happen. I was determined to make it happen for her. I didn't care what I had to do. I was going to make her be Mrs. Conway.

Here it was, the day was here. Mesha was

ready. However, I wasn't. Somehow, she had obtained all the dresses that she needed. Her aunt had already given her a wedding dress. I still needed tuxedos. My mother calls me. I invited her to the wedding even though she had caused me so much pain. I didn't want her to miss what was probably going to be one of the biggest events to take place in her life. While sitting on the sofa in the living room, in a deep thought, the phone rang. "Hello,"

"What are you going to do?" My mother asked.

"I'm getting married today." I told my mother. "I'm not canceling my wedding."

"Get ready, your sister is going to take you to Texarkana." my mother said.

I didn't know what was going to happen. I made some phone calls and told everyone that the wedding was going to happen. My sister picked me up. We drove 45-minutes to Texarkana to the wedding place. Veneka and I got out of the car and went inside.

"How may I help you today?" the woman asked.

"I need some tuxedos for my wedding." I told her, looking around the store.

"When is your big day?" she asked.

"Today,"

"Oh my God!" The woman said, "What size?"

It dawned on me, I never sized the groomsmen.

"That, I don't know." I told her.

"Follow me," she said, "you'll just have to eyeball the men's sizes." I did just that. I carried all the tuxedos to the counter. The cashier told me the total. I wrote a check.

"We can't accept these." The cashier said. She explained to me why. It was something about temporary checks. I walked out the store and got in the car.

"What's wrong?" My sister asked, looking confused.

"They wouldn't accept the check." I told her. Veneka got out of the car and went inside the store. She came back a few minutes later carrying the tuxedos. I didn't ask any questions. I later found out that she wrote a hot check to get them. We started back to Nashville. I made more phone calls.

The next thing I knew, I was sitting beside my uncle J.D., at the church in the pastor's office.

"Don't get nervous now. You're here. It's too late to turn around." My uncle joked with me. I looked at him and cracked a smile.

"It's time," the pastor informed us.

My uncle and I walked inside and took our places. Everyone else was already set. The piano began to play and a woman began to sing. The doors opened and the wedding was on. My uncle looked at me and smiled. My brother and cousin teased me.

Here she comes. My future wife stepped into

my view. She was beautiful. She was being escorted by her biological father. When they made it to me, I grabbed her by the hand and we took our place. I was so overwhelmed until I had slipped into another zone. It was now my turn.

"Do you Byron take Mesha to be your lawfully wedded wife?" The pastor asked me.

"I do," I replied.

"I now pronounce you Mr. and Mrs. Byron Ladavid Conway. You may kiss your bride."

I pulled Mesha to me and kissed her. We turned around to the audience and were greeted with a standing ovation. We were congratulated and hugged by family and friends.

My sister chauffeured us to the wedding reception in her car. People that didn't attend the wedding greeted us at the wedding reception. The lady that made our wedding cake was there also. She had the cake already set up. She greeted us as we went inside. The ladies came and took Mesha away from me. My step father-in-law, Mick, took me outside. He parked his truck directly in front of the building. He smoked joint after joint with me. He went back inside, leaving me with a couple of his favorite beers: Busch's Natural Ice 5.7%. I sat in the driver's seat of Mick's truck. Listening to my favorite song on a CD that Mesha had recently purchased for me. I had "Dilemma" by Nelly featuring Kelly Rowland on repeat. I was higher than the antenna on top of Heaven's television. I looked up and noticed that the wedding cake lady was still there. I already knew why. Mesha and I hadn't paid the lady for the cake. She needed her money. One of our mothers paid the lady. Then she left. I soon was being requested to come in the building. I got out of the truck and went inside the building. People were standing around, chatting. Most were dancing. I looked up and saw the craziest thing. My brother was dancing with my mother-in-law. I knew then that our families were enjoying this day. However, the family ties would soon come to pass.

It was time to dance with my new wife. We danced to the song, "Dilemma." I felt someone tap me on my shoulder.

"Byron, some people want you outside." The girl told me. I went outside and looked around. I finally located who they were. They were my favorite cousins, Priscilla and Randy from Texarkana. I went to greet them. Randy held up a bottle of wine.

"Congratulations cousin," Priscilla said, while hugging me.

"I wasn't expecting y'all to be here." I told them.

"You're family." Randy said.

"So, where is she?" Priscilla asked.

"She's in there probably missing me." I said.

"Boy you are still crazy," Priscilla said to me. We went back in the building. I introduced Priscilla and Randy to Mesha. We made a toast, and then cut the cake. It was getting late. It was time to close the building that we had rented. The mother suggested that we continued the celebration to the parking lot where Mesha and I lived. We were greeted by even more friends when we made it there. My friend got me higher than I already was. Mick continued where they left off. It was dark outside now. Mick had his truck backed in with both doors open and the music playing. He played Sir Charles Jones CD, "Love Machine." I was enjoying this day with my new wife. I was enjoying that day so much and was so intoxicated until I didn't even notice that my sister-in-law, Nita, was spoon-feeding me straight icing off the wedding cake like I was a baby. I couldn't take it anymore. I slipped away from the crowd. I went inside our apartment and flopped on the bed, tuxedo still on. I was so high until my eyes were closed and the room was still spinning. Mesha must have noticed my absence. I could hear her and Trael calling my name.

"Hanh," was all I could get out. They laughed at me. Trael slapped me on the leg.

"I'll see you tomorrow brother-in-law." he said.

"I'm fixing to put him to bed." Mesha said to Trael.

"I bet you are," Trael said with a smug look on his face.

"Trael, get your crazy butt out of here." Trael left out the door. Mesha began taking my clothes off. This is the happiest day of my life, was the last thing I thought before I passed out.

Now every man usually has sex with his new bride on his wedding night. Well, not me. I was too high and intoxicated to do so. I woke up the next morning and turned over to see my new wife. She was turned on her side with her head propped up on her hand, smiling at me. I already knew what time it was. I had some making up to do.

# 7
# Satan Comes To Destroy

Satan comes to destroy. Ever since the "Fall of Man" he continued to carry out his plan to destroy what God created; Man. I was on his personal hit-list.

## "Satan's Destroy Hit List"
1. Byron Conway
2.
3.
4.
5.

My name had been placed at the bottom of his list since his prior attempts to destroy me had already failed. His soldier had informed his of my life's progress. I was doing too much and he had to do something about it. He was back to destroy.

Marriage life was great for Mesha and me. We were making ends meet. We had strong support from family and friends. I still didn't have a job, but Mesha did, working at a nursing home. I did little odd jobs here and there to help pay the bills. Things weren't like we wanted it to be financially but we had what was most important. We had each other and we had love.

Throughout history, there were many other people that Satan tried to destroy. Such as: Joseph, Moses, David, Jesus Christ, the Apostle Paul. Why? Because he knew that they, one day, would be a threat to his kingdom and a soldier for God's kingdom.

Satan knows exactly what to use against anyone one that threatened his kingdom and he know exactly when to do it. He knows our weaknesses. He knew exactly which one to use on me. I was sitting at home one day. Mesha came home from work, crying. Something wasn't right about my wife. I needed to know what it was.
"Bae, what's wrong with you?" I asked.
"You wouldn't believe who I saw today," she said.
"Who?" I asked her.
"Lacy," she told me. I headed straight for the bedroom. I grabbed my pistol and a bag of marijuana. I rolled a blunt. I put both in my backpack and headed out the door for Lacy's

mother's house. I had already told Mesha about this. Because of her kind-heart she still acknowledged my mother. Really on the account of me. The situation had already begun to affect my marriage. One day, we both decided that I needed to see someone about my mental health.

She scheduled an appointment for me. She accompanied me during the visit. I told the people about the conspiracy deal involving my mother. They asked me and my wife many questions. That day, they put me on Prozac and some more medications. I was curious about the situation. One day, I went to talk to the sheriff. He told me to go home and stay there until he called. A few days later, I received a call from him asking me to come down to the station. He met me in the lobby and escorted me to his office. There stood two men dressed in suits, wearing cowboy hats. They introduced themselves and asked me to tell them about the conspiracy. What they said next stunned me.
"Byron, we're going to put your mother and Lacy under federal investigation for "Conspiracy to Commit Murder. We're going to have our branch of the FBI in Oklahoma to pick Lacy up and extradite Lacy back to Arkansas." The FBI agent told me. I was speechless. I went back home and told Mesha.

I lay in the bed for days. I was so bad off

mentally until Mesha had to do all the thinking for me. She came in the bedroom and lay down with me, running her hands through my hair. She stared in my eyes.

"Bae, I know that you're hurting right now, but you need to call them people and tell them that you want them to cancel that investigation." Mesha said, "She's your mother."

I laid there for a moment. I rolled over, grabbed the phone and called the sheriff. I canceled the investigation.

When I made it to Lacy's mother's house, his mother, father, and him were standing in the yard talking. I walked up to them and said hello.

"Lacy, can I talk to you for a minute, in private?" I asked him.

"Yeah bro, I already know what you want to talk about." he said. His mother did too. I had already talked to her about the situation. She pretended to not know of Lacy's whereabouts at the time. I didn't blame her for protecting her son. It was never my intention to get him into any trouble. I only wanted to know the truth. His father was drunk and wanted to play. Lacy's mother grabbed her husband, playfully, but with authority by the shirt and pulled him inside the house. Lacy and I went inside his father's tool shed. I fired up the blunt and we passed it back and forth.

"Bro, I only have two questions for you. One, is it true?" I asked him.

He told me that same exact story as my sister did. "Why didn't you do it?" I asked him the second question.

He removed the blunt from his lips. He was silent for a few seconds then replied.

"Because God wouldn't have wanted me to," he said, passing me the blunt. Tears welled up in my eyes. I passed the blunt back to him, gave him a hug, and then walked out of the shed. I couldn't hold back the pain. I cried all the way home. Satan knew what to use to tear me down. He succeeded.

# 8
# Nadia

Married life was different, but amazing. It made me feel like a king. I knew that I now had a wife to take care of. And I was going to do it by all means necessary. My first thought was to get a job. I also wanted to write another motion picture screenplay.

One day, I told Mesha to go to Wal-Mart and buy me a writing tablet and stop by the weed man house and buy me an ounce of weed. She did what I asked her to. I sat in our spare bedroom and wrote the screenplay. I started on a Monday and finished it that Friday. The only time Mesha interrupted me was when she brought me a plate of food.

Weeks later, I was randomly searching through the yellow pages of the Texarkana phone book. I see "Motion Picture Director." That's odd I thought. I called him up and told him about the screenplay. He told me to get it typed and to send him a copy.

Mesha and I knew where to type the screenplay. We went to the local college. Come to find out, my classmate was over the computer lab. The three of us sat side-by-side and typed the screenplay. It didn't matter what part we typed, my classmate, Steph, knew how to put it in order. I mailed a copy to the director. I knew that I didn't want to live in the projects forever. I wanted a better life for Mesha. I wanted her to have all the things that the average woman would want out of life. I thought about attending college. I wanted to do auto body work and own my own body shop. So, I went to the college and applied for a Pell grant. I called and called to the college to check on the status of my grant application. Finally, one day, I received a call from the college informing me that the Pell grant application was approved.
Satan, the adversary, didn't like that. He knew that he had to make another attempt to throw me off. He knew that he couldn't kill me. So, he made another attempt to destroy me.

My homeboy and I, because of the trades that we chose, had to drive to the campus in Dequeen. Neither one of us had a job, so gas money was hard to come by. I remember one day we stopped to get some gas. I pulled out some rolls of pennies that Mesha had rolled for me and sat them on the counter. The cashier looked at me with a can't-be-serious look on her face.

I received my Pell grant check. It was $1,195.00. Satan had thrown his bait. I took it. Satan will use different things at different times. He does this because people are ignorant to his tactics. Instead of spending my time and money on Mesha, I hit the streets with a pocket full of money. No exact destination in mind. I ended up interacting with some people that I never interacted with. "Everything is on me" was how the day ended.

The next day, I was being accused of rape. I panicked and went on the run. Two days later, my mother caught up with me via telephone.
"Momma, I haven't raped anybody." I told her.
"Then why are you running?" she asked me.
"I don't know," I said.
"The investigator said that if you didn't do it come back and he'll help you." Momma said.
I thought about it. My aunt drove me back to Nashville in the snow. The next morning the investigator drove me to the Hempstead County Jail in Hope, Arkansas, my birthplace. My home. I was given a computerized voice stress analysis test. I never heard anything else about the case. Satan wasn't done yet. He was throwing everything in his "book of destroying" at me. He had to shut

me down. He came up with a different scheme.

My family and Mesha's family became enemies. Satan was using them. They caused more strife than the Hatfield's and McCoy's. I was trapped in the middle. They were driving me crazy. My college instructor sent me a message to come back to college. I went back for a day or two, but couldn't handle it. I never went back. I was losing my mind. I had to get back on my medications. It seemed like every time my wife left and came home, she had had a conflict with my mother, sister, and brother.

My wife never caused any trouble. It was more of a jealousy thing on their part. I was spending all my time with my wife.
I remember one day; I went down to my mother's house. My sister asked me to ride somewhere with her. We got in the car. My sister told me that she would buy me a car if I would divorce my wife. That wasn't an option.

After that, it was all about Mesha. We still lived in the projects. We were enjoying our life together. I kicked it more with my brother-in-laws, Trael and Bug. Mesha and I normally shared our weekends with her mother and her husband, Mick. We would always watch her favorite Tyler Perry's "Madea" stage plays. This is how I later became a big Tyler Perry fan. I like Tyler Perry because his stories were based on real life. Everyday life.

One Monday came around. I was out front of the apartment planting some seeds. I looked up and the same investigator came around the corner. "Good morning, Byron." He greeted me. "Can you go down to the station with me?" "Yes sir," I said. I went inside and told Mesha what was going on. I grabbed my wallet and followed the investigator to his car. He drove us to his office. We went inside. "Byron, Anthony Stuart said that you put his girlfriend's, Carolyn, car tires on flat." The investigator informed me. l "Man, I haven't put nobody tires on flat." I told him looking angry. By that time, I heard some car doors slamming. My wife and mother came storming into the office. "Y'all need to let him go," my mother raged. I had never known my mother to act this way about me. Never. I knew something was wrong, but couldn't put my finger on it. My wife and I put it together weeks later.

One even I came home from riding horses with my friend, Darrell. I passed out in bed. My wife said that my mother unexpectedly popped up. She told my wife that she would be back in a minute. She left and returned minutes later. Then quickly left. My mother was the one who sliced Carolyn's tires.

Carolyn and my mother were enemies. They shared a man. Which, in fact, was Anthony. Carolyn lived in the same projects as I did. So, I was the first to blame because I was the son of his other woman. There was no evidence nor eye witnesses. So the investigator let me go. I went home. I thought about the situation all day. Satan had me right where he wanted me. I was losing my mind and didn't even realize it.

I woke up the next morning thinking about how Anthony had falsely accused me of something that I didn't have anything to do with. I was "bad mad." I wanted to confront Anthony. I grabbed my glock and a couple of blunts and headed out the door to where I knew he was. My mother's house. I knew his routine like I did the back of my hand because he and my mother had been messing around since 1994.

I see my uncle Tony sitting on my aunt's porch. I stopped and sat beside my uncle. I fired the blunt up. I smoked about three-quarters of it with him. I hit the blunt one more time, passed it to him, then took off walking towards my mother's house. She only lived a couple hundred feet away.
I walked in the yard, straight over to her bedroom window. I took the butt of the glock and knocked very hard on her window.
"Come on out of there, nigga. I know you're in there." I barked. I got ready to knock again, but

was interrupted.

"Boy, what's wrong with you?" I heard my mother's words.

"Tell that nigga to come on outta there. I'm fixing to handle him." I told my mother. Once again God took control.

"Boy, go home to your wife." My mother said.

"Man, I'm not playing," I said, pulling the glock from inside my waist and showing it to her.

"I'm fixing to call your parole officer," my mother said as she was turning to go back inside the house.

God intervened. He prevented me from making the same mistake that my father had done. I took off running down the street. I was mad and hurt at the same time because I was falsely accused by a man that I once looked up to and at the same time, my mother was protecting him.

I knew that my parole officer would be looking for me soon. I ran to a friend's house and hid the glock under the house. By the time I walked back to the front, the investigator and my parole officer pulled up with more police. They searched me, then let me go.

If God wouldn't have intervened then, I would've thrown my life away. I knew that I had to get out of Nashville. I got some clothes from my friend, Bo-leg. Bo-leg was my teenage years' best friend. When you saw one of us, the other one was somewhere around. We were the neighborhood "BMX Bandits." We could pop a wheelie and go from one street corner to another. Plus, he was like my childhood brother-in-law. I used to go with his sister, Gendell, like 10-times.

I had a female friend to take me to Texarkana. I basically hitchhiked. I just up and left. I didn't bother to tell Mesha. I had forgot about my medications. It wasn't working anyway. I made it to my aunt, Nae's house. She was my great aunt. I mingled with family for a while. I loved to spend time with my family in Texarkana because I only saw them a few times a year. They were down to earth and loved to have family gatherings. It's hundreds of them, literally hundreds. They loved to see me. They would take me from one family members house to another. My uncle Elaine was one of my favorite He thought that he was cooler than an Alaskan Eskimo sitting on an Arctic iceberg butt-booty naked.

My aunt let me know that I had a cousin that stayed down the road. They gave me the directions on how to get there. I walked down the summer-hot street with my hair braided to the back, red and white beads hanging on the ends, a red bandanna tied around the front of my forehead. I was wearing my black Nike's, blue jean shorts, with a red shirt that read "1000 Stud Fee" in big white letters.

I made it to the location in minutes. It was a set of government housing projects. I walked through the open gate.
"Damn, he fine." I heard someone say. I looked in the direction that the voice came from. I noticed four or five women sitting on a porch. I made it to my cousin, Linda's place. I knocked on the door. She was happy to see me. She called for her fiancé so that I could meet him. Come to find out, me and her fiancé was in a foster home together years ago. I stayed there until the sun went down. I knew that my aunt was worrying about me. I said my goodbyes.

I was walking on my way out the projects and heard someone say something that alerted me.
"Ima kill that nigga right there." I heard the voice say. I stopped. I reached for the glock as I slowly turned. I had my target in sight
"Boy, put that damn gun down and come give me a hug," the person said.
It was my friend, Terry. He was a friend that I met while staying with a female friend in Bradley, Arkansas. We also done some time together at the Grimes Unit.
He walked up to me and hugged me. It was good to see that he was doing good. He seemed like he hadn't seen me in ten years.
"Come on, bro. I want to take you to meet my

girl." he said. We walked about three apartments down. He opened the door of the apartment and walked in. A short dark-skinned female with a young boy was sitting on the couch. He introduced us.

I stayed for a while then went back up to my aunt Nae's place. I woke up the next morning, got myself together and went back to Terry's. I would eventually form a routine of this.

One evening, I went to my aunt's, Mesha had called. She was worried about me and so was my aunt.

I was far gone, mentally. I didn't care if I lived or died. My family, both sides, but mostly mine had drove me insane. I didn't have no intentions on going back home. I was headed for self-destruction.

Every day, Terry and his girlfriend was coming to me telling me that this or that female wanted to get with me. I was a new face in a new place and all the females wanted me first.

I started drinking alcohol and smoking weed heavily. I even smoked and drank alcohol with strangers. I could see a group of people and just walk up in the crowd and accept whatever drugs or alcohol that they had. They could have easily killed me and gotten away with it. It wouldn't have mattered. My own mother wanted to kill me. So what would have been the difference if a stranger had done the job.

Terry ended up going to jail for leaving the halfway house that he had paroled to. I don't know how I escaped "the NCIC" search. The police ran all of our names. I was on parole in another county. That's residential traveling. That was an easy violation.

I had continued to stay with Terry's girlfriend. I never tried to get with her or nothing like that. I still had some morals even though I was losing my mind. I don't sleep with family or friend's girlfriends nor exes.

I started kicking it with a dude named B. He repped the same thing that I did. All he did was babysit his son while his fiancé was gone to work. We smoked weed and played the game all day. The game really played me, because I would try to get higher and higher. However, that wouldn't stop my mind from thinking about the war that was going on back home.

Every day, I would stay at B's till late. Then I would go back to Kay's place. She would be waiting on me with, "Such and such want to holler at you." Females were coming at me from all directions. They were adding to the stress. I finally

got tired and that lil devil said, "If you sleep with them, they'll leave you alone."
I had sex with one black female and one white female.

One night, I stayed at B's till late. I knew that I had to get back to Kay's place. I went to the apartment and knocked on the door. Kay, finally opened it after a few knocks. I went in and sat on the couch in pitch black darkness I didn't know if I was going or coming. I wanted to die.

A knock at the back door shattered my thoughts. I sat there a minute before I decided to go to the door. I didn't want the "knocker" to wake Kay up. I walked to the back door and opened it. There stood this short light-skin female looking up at me.
"Come go with me," she said, grabbing my hand.

She led me a couple of apartments down and we sat on the concrete porch. She took my hand and placed it on the crouch of her pants. She noticed that I wasn't really feeling in the mood. "I'll be back. Stay right here." she said. She left and came back minutes later. She took my hand and replaced it back in the same spot. There was something different this time I could feel her flesh. I rubbed her vagina, then stopped. I wasn't in the mood. She grabbed my hand.
"Come on," she said, leading me further away

from Kay's apartment.

She led me to an apartment. She led me up a flight of stairs. It was dark and music was playing. I could tell that other people were in the room. She left and came back. She handed me a glass with something in it. I didn't care what it was. I was drinking it.

The female gave me a lap dance. She grabbed my hand again, then led me into a bedroom. She unbuttoned my pants, pulled my penis out and stroked it until I gained an erection. The door opened while we were having sex. We both looked back at the same time. A woman stood in the doorway. She didn't say anything. She closed the door.

My light-skin admirer went and got a wet towel. She came back and cleaned the both of us. She led me back to the door. I went back to Kay's place, set up in the dark until I fell asleep.

The next morning, I got up and got ready to go to B's house. There was a knock at the door. I opened the door. There stood two females. "Here," she said, handing me a piece of folded paper. "Are you Nadia's boyfriend?" "Who?" I said while reaching for the paper. "Nothing," the female said. They walked off. I didn't think nothing of the folded paper. I threw it on the table and went up to B's place.

The next morning, something wasn't right. Kay asked me to leave. I called my aunt. Two of my cousins came and got me. I stayed with one of them until he came home late one night and found me passed out on his porch with the glock laying on my chest. They knew then that they had to get me back home. God had sent his angels to get me.

# 9
# The Arrest

I was back at home and all hell had broken lose. Things were worst now than they were before. I didn't tell Mesha about my Texarkana episode. She was too excited about me being home.

Summer was coming in. One evening, I went to ride horses with Darrell. We sat on his porch when we came back. Soon I heard some people arguing a block away. The voice sounded familiar. It was Mesha's voice. I took off running with Darrell following me. I made it around the corner and noticed my sister-in-law's car and my mother's car parked in one of my female's friend front yard. My wide and sister-in-law were arguing with my sister and brother. When my brother started talking crazy to me. He had a kitchen knife. He acted as if he wanted to run up on me. Someone grabbed him. "Let him go," I said. "Come on momma's boy." I made Mesha and my sister-in-law go home. I went home also. Things were out of control. I was stressed and exhausted. I left home again. I went stayed with a friend in the country. I thought that if I left, my family would leave Mesha alone. She wanted to spend some time together on our first anniversary. She cried as I made love to her. I finally moved back home. I got very bad, mentally. For the sake of our marriage, Mesha and I decided that I needed to go back to seeing mental health. I did.

My father came home from prison. I went to go see him. When I came back, Mesha was crying. "Bae, what's wrong with you?" I asked her. She didn't want to tell me at first. I asked her again. "Bae, what's wrong with you?" I asked her again, giving her that husband look.
"Your brother jumped on me," she said.
"My brother did what?" I asked her again.
"Your brother jumped on me," she said, crying even harder. I went nuts. She explained what happened. She decided to go visit her mom at her new home which was a hundred yards up the street. My brother pulled up beside her, got out of the car and attacked. Luckily, she was right in front of her mother's house. Her brother ran out the house and beat my brother. I couldn't take it no more. I looked for mental health to help me. They nor the medication could help.

One day, I went to mental health and said some "what if" things. The next thing I know I was being labeled as a menace to society and being told that I was going to be put in jail until I went to the state hospital. I was so mad that I walked over to the jail myself. Mesha was hysterical. They put me in a cell until a bed at the state hospital finally came available for me. I made it to the hospital. I was evaluated and placed on more medications.

On the thirteenth day, I received an emergency phone call. I grabbed the receiver.
"Hello," I said.
"Bae," Mesha said, crying.
"Bae, what's wrong?" I asked her.
"Bae, everything we own is burning up in a house fire." she cried. I stayed on the phone with her for a while. I told the nursed what was going on. I talked to the doctor. He discharged me the next day. A friend drove Mesha to Little Rock to pick me up. She was excited to see me. Another friend named Gerald gave us $300.00 to help us out. A man that owned some rent houses allowed my mother-in-law, Mick, Mesha, and I to stay in one of his rent houses for free. I, now, was taking 3,003mg of mental health meds a day.
Mesha found a job at the new Wal-Mart. Soon we had our own house. Mental health had me "balanced." However, it was too late. Satan had already caused the damage.

On March 6, 2004 I was sitting on our porch with our pit bull, Butterscotch." A county sheriff car hit the corner. I didn't think anything of it. It stopped right in front of the house. Two officers departed the cruiser

"Byron," one of the officers said.

"You know anything about Hempstead County having a misdemeanor warrant?" The officer asked.

"Yeah, it's old." I said. Back in 2000, I was in Hope one day. I was walking to the corner store. A cop car pulled up beside me. I gave him a fake name. I ended up going to jail that day for criminal mischief.

Mesha came outside. She was crying her heart out. I gave her my wallet and keys. I told her that it was just a misdemeanor and that I was going to lay the fine out. So I thought. The deputies didn't know what was really going on. Neither did I. The officers walked me towards the car.

"Please, Y'all don't take him. Please," Mesha cried.

"Bae, I'm going to be okay," I assured her.

"No, Bae. Please don't go," she cried some more. I blew her a kiss and got in the backseat of the cruiser. No handcuffs. On the way to the station the officers talked as if they were never going to see me again.

"Byron, you want a cigarette?" One of the officers asked.

"Sure," I said. The officer in the passenger seat lit

a cigarette and passed it back to me. I puffed on the cigarette until we made it to the station. We went in through the front. All the staff were speaking to me. The deputies escorted me to the booking room, then left.

A few minutes later, the sheriff walked out. He reminds you of Hoss Cartwright from the western, "Bonanza."

"Byron," he said, "You know Miller County has a rape warrant for your arrest?"

"I haven't raped nobody." I said.

"Calm down," he said, "I know you haven't raped nobody. I've been knowing you a long time. It's something about an underage female." He explained to me that the legislation had added an age clause to the class "Y" rape felony.

Miller County was supposed to come and get me, but called and said that it would be the next day. The county dressed me out and took me to a housing pod. I sat at a table thinking about who the female could be. And thinking about Mesha. Satan had accomplished his task.

# 10
# The Hardest Decision That I Ever Had To Make

I wrote Mesha and told her the truth about everything. By her being the loving, caring, and understanding woman that she was, she remained by my side.

I was extradited to the Bi-State Justice Building in Texarkana. I was placed in an observation tank by myself because I was on medications. Mesha made sure that I had them before I left Nashville.

The next day, I was interrogated by a pregnant Caucasian woman. She asked me what happened while I was in Texarkana. I told her exactly what happened. She wanted to know who the woman was that was standing in the doorway that night. I told her that I didn't know. She told me about a letter that Nadia had written to me. It was the letter that the two females delivered to me that morning.

Yeah, the one that I didn't think nothing of. The one that I threw on the table. That's what got me. She also told me that Nadia was only twelve years old. I was crushed.

I was transferred to the Miller County Jail. Once I got settled in, I talked to a few of the guys in there. I told them what had happened. They got mad and said that I shouldn't have been in jail. They knew Nadia and her mother's lifestyle. I was appointed a public defender. I pleaded not guilty by reason of mental disease or defect. I surely didn't want to live no more by now.

One night, I waited until everybody went to sleep. I took my sheet and went hung myself from the door jamb rod. Some guys heard the box break up under me. They ran to the back where I was and held me up until staff made it there. I spent my twenty-fifth birthday on suicide watch. I was sent back to prison on my parole violation. Mesha was still by my side. I received letters from her every week. I went back and forth to court. My public defender never tried to help me build a case. the only one thing that he done right was requested a mental evaluation. I went back to take the evaluation. The psychologist acted as if he didn't believe that I went through everything that I told him about. He said that he was going to call my grandmother and verify the events. He never did. I self-incriminated myself during the evaluation.

Something my lawyer never told me about.

On court day, I reviewed the evaluation report. The results had stated that I had mental disease but not mental defect. It also said that I said that I knew what I did was wrong. The doctor worded it how it would benefit the state. When the doctor asked me the question, I told them that I thought what I had did was wrong now because eighteen months had elapsed since the incident and the evaluation. My state of mind during the time of the incident was at a diminished capacity. That's what they were supposed to go by.

By me being a two-time convicted felon being accused of a sexual offense with a public defender who didn't want to fight for me, I was forced to plead out. I agreed to a reduced felony of second degree sexual assault and a 15-year sentence. I filed a Rule 37 appeal. It was denied. I knew that I was in it for the long haul. I did my 60-day initial assignment, then I requested to go to vo-tech. I chose Food Service Technology. I had to do a total of 50 months on the 15-year sentence. I was going to make a way even though I was in prison. So I thought.

One night, I received a letter from Mesha. Trael had been shot in the neck and was paralyzed. Here comes Satan messing with my head. I knew that I had a couple of years to do. I loved

Mesha with all my heart and wanted the best for her. I knew that she would eventually need some help. I knew that she had needs that I wasn't going to be able to fulfill for four years.

I made the hardest decision that I've ever had to make. I wrote Mesha and told her that I wanted a divorce. I thought that was the right thing to do at the time. I didn't know that Jesus had told the Pharisees:

*"What therefore God hath joined together, let not man put asunder."* -Matthew 19:6

See sometimes when we make decisions in life, we make them out of selfishness, not knowing that the decisions we don't have to make them for ourselves, but also take into account the best interest of the ones that love us also.

# 11
# Saved

I was lost. I didn't know what direction to go in. I felt like I was in this world all alone. I felt empty inside, betrayed and heartbroken. I didn't know what Mesha's response was going to be. Everything seemed to bother me. I had accumulated about 400-hours of the 1,440-hours that's needed to complete vo-tech.

One day, I felt as if my supervisor was picking on me. I went into a rage. He told me to go back to the barrack. A couple of days later, I received a major disciplinary. The disciplinary hearing officer reduced me to class four. I was moved to the class four barracks. I was in bad shape. Not in as bad of a shape as I was when I was sent back to start doing my parole violation.

I remember when I first made it back, I was down for the count. The mental health medication had me spiritually dead. I laid in bed for days. I didn't go eat. I didn't go to the shower. My friends tried to get me out of bed to go to yard call. I just didn't have it I me.

Here it was a year later. I was bad off just not as bad as I was a year ago. I finally received a response letter from Mesha. The envelope had "No Divorce" written all over the front and back of the envelope. I read the letter. She was upset and heartbroken at the same time. I could tell that she had mixed emotions. It wasn't what she wanted. It really wasn't what I wanted either. But I did it. I couldn't see any light. All I could see was darkness. Pitch black darkness. It was as if I walked around every day with my eyes closed.

I remember one night the officer on the door called "church call." I didn't usually go to church. However, something told me to go this night. I followed the crowd of inmates to the chapel. I sat in the middle. I looked around. Then it seemed as if what the preacher was saying was directed at me.

A man got up and sang a song called "Heavenly Choir." I felt a little bit better. They had altered call. One again, something told me to go. When I made it to the front, I asked the man how could I be saved. He told me the same thing that the apostle Paul told the Romans:

*"That if thou shalt confess with thy mouth the Lord Jesus, and shalt believe in thine heart that God hath raised him from the dead, thou shalt be saved."*     -Romans 10:9

That night, I got saved. A few months later, Mesha and my divorce was finalized.

# 12

# The Beginning of a
# Restoration Processing

It was now 2006. I was incarcerated for two years now. I was being housed at the Ouachita River Correctional Unit at Malvern, Arkansas. I had been saved for a year at this point. I had already given up on God. Satan had control of my mental health. I was still taking the psychotropic medications. The medication did more harm than it done good. I was chemically dependent.

A man's heart being filled with greed and lust would never tell you that the medication would help one problem, but wouldn't tell you that it would cause a person ten other problems. So now we're having to take more medications for those additional problems known as "side effects." I learned one important thing between "side effects." She there's a difference between "God's Medication" (the word of God) and man's medication (pills). We have to pay for man's medication. God's medication is "free." Man's medication has negative side effects. While God's medication has only positive side effects.

I was bad off. I lashed out at friends. I wrote bad letters home. Every day I had confrontations with staff. They didn't know what was going on. I was like "a bomb." When I blew up, I destroyed everything around me, including friends. There were many times when I had to go back and apologize for the damage that I had caused. Some understood and some didn't.

I confided in people from all walks of life. Family, friends, doctors, teachers, counselors, prison guards, inmates, etc... No one had the answers to my questions.

1. Why did my mother try to have me killed?
2. Why don't my family love me?
3. What did the county court violate my constitutional rights?
4. Why did my brother-in-law have to be paralyzed?
5. Why was I abused so much?

These were just some of my questions. I was outraged at "man" because no one had the answers. I wanted my life back. I made up my mind to take it back. We "as human beings" often expect a helping hand, someone to help us first. So we sit around and have our own "pity party." I had to stop feeling sorry for myself. I had to do something. I wanted back what Satan had taken from me. My mind. I didn't wait and depend on man anymore. I did as 'the prodigal son" son had done. I turned back to my father. I took the first step.

*"Seek ye first the Kingdom of God, and his righteousness; and all these things shall be added unto you."* -Matthew 6:33

I pray to God and repented of my sins. I asked God to restore my mind.

*"Ask, and it shall be given to you; seek, and ye shall find; knock, and it shall be opened unto you: For everyone that ask receiveth; and he that seeketh findeth; and to him that knocketh it shall be opened."*

-Matthew 7:7-8

I didn't think that it was possible for a man to overcome a brain injury. Most people don't. That's because they were putting their trust in "man." I learned to put my trust in God. Jesus told his disciples this:

*"With men this is impossible; but with God all things are possible."* -Matthew 19:26

God started his restoration process. He weaned me off of man's medication; pills. And prescribed me his medication; his word.
This happened because of a process that I had to take. I had to take the following steps:

1. Repent of my sins.
2. Ask God for what I wanted.
3. I had faith that he was going to keep his word.

God has been the same since the beginning. There were many people that he restored something to.
He restored the following:

- Abraham his <u>wife</u> Sarah (Genesis 20:14)
- Chief Butler unto his <u>position</u> (Genesis 40:21)
- Joseph unto his <u>office</u> (Genesis 41:13)
- King Jeroboam his <u>hand</u> (1 Kings 13:6)
- A man's right <u>hand</u> (Matthew 21:13)
- A blind man his <u>sight</u> (Mark 8:22-25)

It didn't matter what the case was. God made it happen. He was making it happen for me.

# 13
# Chosen

I sat in my one-man cell at the Grimes Unit. It was now July 2012. I had backslid in my faith and gave up on God for the second time. Satan was back in control.

I had been involved in a bad situation with an officer. I was lost and confused. I needed some direction. I turned back to man. That's how I lost my focus on God.

The institution bounced me from unit to unit because of paperwork and lawsuits that I was filing. I never thought that I would learn the law in prison. This was part of God turning a bad situation into a good one.

After the incident with the officer, I went through an "over-generalization phase." All officers were the same. That's how I saw things and no one could tell me anything different.

The unit's administration had put me on "staff alert" because of some things that I said in a letter that I wrote to my grandmother. I had accumulated eighteen months of punitive isolation days. I had more than the "inner me" as an enemy. One of the wardens was my enemy also. Every time he came by my cell, I lashed out at him. He would have whoever the escorting officer that was with him to write me a major disciplinary. I was at the bottom of the barrel. I spent majority of my day reading case law. Every now and then, I would go stand at the door and talk to other inmates. They were going through the same thing that I was. We talked about all types of things from sports to politics. I was the Johnnie Cochran of the segregation. Every man that needed legal help came to me.

I felt as if my family had stop believing in me. The problem was I had stop believing in myself. I had stop believing that anything was possible with God. I had stop believing that God was a comforting God. What I did believe is that my enemies had me beat.

Sometimes Satan has us down so much until we don't even recognize that the only other way to go is "up." The first step to doing that is to look in that direction, up. You have to look "up" to God and allow him to see that we not only need a helping hand, but that we are looking to turn back to him. I needed something different. I was going around in circles. I was on the verge of losing my mental health again until God intervened.

On July 2011, I sat on my bed doing some legal work. The officer slid a letter under my door. It was from my sister, Veneka. I read the letter. I started crying. I grabbed some paper and a pen and wrote her back. I explained to her that I knew that she had something to do with the conspiracy, the murder plot. Satan had control of her mind at the time.

That was my mother's Plan C, after Plan A and Plan B failed. My sister didn't think that I knew what was going on.

One day after Plan A and Plan B failed, my sister called me down to my mother's house. I knocked on the door.
"Come in," my sister said. She was sitting on the arm of the couch across from me. My mother came up the hallway and went out the door without looking nor speaking to me. I knew something was wrong. My sister, out of the blue, pulled a .380 pistol on me. She was talking crazy. I was confused. When it got time for her to take me out, God took control over her mind from Satan for a split second, and it felt like he pushed me in my back and said, "Go. Now." I got up and hurriedly

rushed out the house. My mother's third and final plan had failed.

I explained to my sister in the letter that the police would've knew that something wasn't right and that she would've most likely went to prison. I sealed the letter and laid down. I laid there crying. Then God gave me more mind restoration. After fourteen years, it came to me. I was there. I was there at the spot where Lacy was supposed to kill me.

After Plan A failed, my mother put me out. One evening Lacey pulled up beside me. He was driving my mother's new car.

"What's up, Bro?" Lacy asked.

"Chilin," I told him.

"What you about to do?"

"Nothing," I replied.

"Come hit a few blocks with me?" he asked. I got in the passenger seat of the car. We made a few blocks in the neighborhood, then he turned out on the highway. He drove to the Buck Range community. He turned off on a dirt road. He drove down the dirt road a couple of hundred feet then he stopped. He looked out in the wooded area, then at me. He looked out in the wooded area again, then back at me. He shook his head, then drove off. God had taken control over his mind.

I cried myself to sleep that night I woke up the next morning. I sat on the side of my bed. It seemed like God was waiting on me to get up so that he could talk to me. It felt like he put his hand on my shoulder.

"Son," God spoke to me.

"I don't want to," I said to God. I was already rebelling before I knew it. But as human beings, that's how we are. We ask or look for something, but when it's time to receive it we be so blind until we don't even recognize the hand that's reaching out to help us.

"Son, I need you to go. I need you to go somewhere for me. I have some people that I need you to help." God said to me. "I have the key." I knew then that I had been chosen by God to do a work for him. God was taking a bad situation and turning it into a good one. It took me thirty-two years to recognize that I was chosen.

*"So the last shall be first, and the first last: for many be called but few chosen."* -Matthew 20:16

Because of the issues that I had had with the warden, I refused classification. The next classification day had come. An officer brought me a refusal sheet as they normally do. He was surprised when I told them that I was going. The put me in four-point restraints and escorted me to classification.

"Conway," the warden said, "Man, you've been doing good. The computer says you've been 4 months without a disciplinary." the warden said, looking at the computer screen.

"Yes sir," I responded.

"Man, we have to get you out that cell," he said, "That cell is bad for you."

Something wasn't right about the warden. He seemed to be nice to me. But the Lord said:

*"When a man's ways please the Lord, he maketh even his enemies to be at peace with him."* - Proverbs 16:7

"Do you believe in God?" The warden asked. The question hit me hard. I started crying.

"No, sir. I used to." I told him.

"Why did you stop believing in him?" he asked.

"Because my mother tried to kill me for some insurance money." I said.

"Well, maybe the chaplain will take you in the pal program." The warden said.

"We'll take a look at it." The chaplain said.

I was escorted back to my cell. The next week, I went back to classification. The most amazing thing happened. The administration took me off staff alert and put me in the program, class four with six-month punitive remaining. I was the first inmate that they had done that for. God had shown his ultimate power. He had the Key to the door.

# 14
# Forgiveness 101

The Pal Program was a faith-based program based on the principles and application of life's skills. It offered studies such as; Life Skills, Men's Fraternity, Money Management, Anger Resolution, Character Qualities, etc...

I had been in there for a couple of weeks. I was falsely accused of being insolent to a staff member because of a grievance that I wrote. I went to disciplinary court and the hearing officer sentenced me to fifteen days' punitive isolation. They put me back in segregation.

The very next day, I went outside for rec call. I was standing in the bullpen talking to the guy next to me. I looked up and saw the chaplain coming through the door on his scooter. I was surprised to see him.

"Byron," he said.

"Yes sir," I answered.

"I don't know what you did to those guys, but they wand you back in there." The chaplain said. I asked myself, what did you do? I know what I did. I shared my story with the guys in there. I touched some hearts. I had done what God had chosen me to do. I was taking my testimony, my hurt, my pain to help others.

The warden came through later that day. I told him what the chaplain said. He told me not to worry about it, that to do the 15 days and he was going to put me back in there.

God now as showing me favor. The warden kept his word. I as placed back in the program. The barracks had already changed around some. So I began doing what I call 3-L'ing: Looking, listening, and learning.

At first, I didn't recognize what the reason why I was in there. So, I was quick to point the finger and notice faults in other people. I wasn't there for them. I was there for me. Like some church people go to church and be quick to say what sister so and so is doing. Or what brother so and so said. One thing I learned was that Jesus didn't come to help the well people, but the sick ones. That's the whole purpose of people going to church and the reason why I had been placed in the program, not by man, but by God because I needed some healing.

Every day I done some litigation work while the instructor talked. I went to him after group one day.
"Can you not talk to a person, but still love them?" I asked Larry Ashley.
"You do be listening, don't you?" He responded.
"Yes, I do," I told him.
"Sure you can love someone and not talk to them."
I had hated my mother for over a decade by now. I really didn't care if she lived or died.

One day, Larry Ashley taught a class on "Forgiveness." I knew then why God had placed me in the program. The program was like a college for me. And I was majoring in "Forgiveness 101." I thought about it for a few days. I came to the conclusion that if I couldn't forgive my mother but God could, then I would be saying that I'm bigger than God. But, I'm not. I, just like you, have also did some wrong things. That's why Jesus said:

*"Judge not, and ye shall not be judged: condemn not, and ye shall not be condemned: forgive, and ye shall be forgiven."*
-Luke   6:37

It took a lot for me to do it. Even though my mother was the wrongdoer, I took the initiative to rebuild a relationship with her. A couple of days before Christmas, I wrote her and sent her a Christmas card. She wrote me back and sent me a Christmas card. She also did a lot of apologizing throughout the letter. Once again, she didn't say what she was apologizing for.

The New Year came in. It was time for me to graduate. Another officer wrote me a disciplinary I went to classification. I was class three at the time. Once again, God showed his power. The warden did something that I had never seen before. He dismissed the disciplinary on the spot, promoted me to class two and assigned me to the Food Service department.

The very next day, I was called for visitation. I had to go make sure that they had the right person, because my family lived over three hours away and had never been to visit. I got dressed and went to visitation. It was my grandmother. God was working.

# 15
# Tested

It was time for me to go up for the parole board again. I had already been denied parole, twice. I had made class one status by remaining disciplinary free for sixty days.

My mother and grandmother drove up to Newport for my parole board hearing. The commissioner told my family and that he would be voting for me to be released. He also told us to take heed that there would be other people voting. I had my supervisor check the computer and see if I had made parole. The parole board deferred my parole until completion of RSVP.

The Reduction of Sexual Victimization Program was a program for inmates whom had been convicted of sexual-related offenses.

I was immediately transferred to the Ouachita River Correctional Unit at Malvern, Arkansas. The only thing that I liked about the unit was that it was only an hour away from home. I could get visits from my family.

God, the first creator known to man, had to test what he re-created. He, like a first inventor, had to test his product.

*"It is impossible but that offenses will come: but woe unto him, through whom they come."*
-Luke 17:1

On the sixth day that I was in the program, a fellow peer pulled me up on an issue. I exploded right there in the middle of group. I signed out of the program. Sometime after, it was told to me that it was a misunderstanding on the other inmate's pact. He thought that I was giving another inmate a hard time, but I wasn't. I was being a "big brother" and giving him words of encouragement. I was written a disciplinary for signing out of the program. The disciplinary hearing officer reduced my class status back to class four.

Many people were tested in the bible. Even Jesus. God allows Satan to test us. Those obstacles are put along our paths for us to face and overcome them so that God can put us in position where he need us to be. However, we turn and run away from that obstacle not knowing that when we get tired of running and turn back around that same obstacle is going to be there because our blessing is on the other side. So, we should learn to face and overcome that obstacle. I ran from mine, forgetting that my blessing was on the other side. Freedom. I was transferred back to the Grimes Unit. I lashed out at an officer a couple of days after I was back. I was placed back in segregation for thirty days. I failed the test. I was tired. I needed some rest.

*"Come unto me, all that that labour and are heavy laden, and I will give you rest."*
-Matthew 11:28

Satan had won that round, but the fight was far from being over. I wasn't going to give up anymore.

# 16
# Principles Applied

It dawned on me why Satan had won another round. I wasn't applying the principles that I learned in the Pal Program, the college of God. There's a difference between reading the bible and applying it. Some people read a couple of verses of the bible and close it only to say that they read the bible. In order for us to overcome O.S.D., Original Sin Disorder, we have to apply God's principles to our daily lives.

Original Sin Disorder is the condition of sin that marks people as a result of Adam's first act of disobedience known as "The Fall of Man." (Genesis Chapter 3)

I, myself, suffered from O.S.D. Because of my disobedience of applying God's principles. God gave Moses the ten main principles known as the Ten Commandments for man to adhere to and live by.

## The Ten Commandments

1. Thou shalt not have no other gods before me (Exodus 20:3)
2. Thou shalt not make unto thee any graven image (Exodus 20:4-5)
3. Thou shalt not take the name of the Lord thy God in vain (Exodus 20:7)
4. Remember the sabbath, to keep it holy (Exodus 20:8-11)
5. Honour thy father and thy mother (Exodus 20:12)
6. Thou shalt not kill (Exodus 20:13)
7. Thou shalt not commit adultery (Exodus 20:14)
8. Thou shalt not steal (Exodus 20:15)
9. Thou shalt not bear false witness against thy neighbor (Exodus 20:16)
10. Thou shalt not covet...anything that is thy neighbors (Exodus 20:17)

God gave man over 2,701- plus laws to live by. The Two Greatest Commandments and the New Commandment was implemented in the new testament.

1. Thou shalt love the Lord thy God with all thy heart, and with all thy soul, and with all thy mind. (Matthew 22:36-38)
2. Thou shalt love thy neighbor as thyself.

(Matthew 22:39)

## The New Commandments

1.  That ye love one another; as I have loved
    you, that ye also love one another. (John
    13:34-35)

I started applying these principles. I was
released from isolation again with two major
disciplinarians pending. Only one was brought up
at my disciplinary court hearing. The hearing
officer found me guilty, sixty days' privileges
restriction.

If I was going to apply God's principles, I
would have to do the opposite of what I was doing.
I had to stop hating prison guards. God made a
way for that to happen. He put me in a position to
where I had to interact with them.

I was assigned back to food service. After a
couple of months, I was promoted to oversee a
kitchen clean-up crew. I had to work directly with
a prison guard. Another set of principles that I had
to apply were the nine fruits of the spirit: love, joy,
peace long suffering, gentleness, goodness, faith,
meekness, and temperance. (Galatians 5:22-23)

I had to meet God halfway. I even had to stop filing lawsuits. I had to get in the passenger's seat and allow God to drive because he knows the way.

The kitchen was inspected every week. Every week, the reports became better. The kitchen was improving. During this course of assignment, I learned how to forgive. I knew how to socialize with staff and inmates.

*"He that handleth a matter wisely shall find good:and who trusteth in the Lord, happy is he."*
-Proverbs 16:20

I was promoted to staff dining after eleven months. The warden that was once my enemy was back at the unit. My supervisor and I didn't know what the warden's response was going to be after seeing me in staff dining. He actually approved it.

One day, the chaplain came in staff dining to eat. The subject came up about me going to the Pal Program and sharing my testimony. This would have to be approved through the same warden. The chaplain returned a few days later. The warden approved the request.

*"A man's gift maketh room for him, and bringeth him before great men."*
-Proverbs 18:16

The event was scheduled. I looked throughout the Pal audience and witnessed many men crying as I shared my testimony. Two wardens and my supervisor were in attendance. After I finished sharing my testimony, one Pal student came up to me crying, hugged and thanked me. He had had a bad experience with his mother as well. The wardens and my supervisor shook my hand and encouraged me to continue speaking. Three months passed by. I sang "Oh Sweet Jesus" with the choir behind me. Then I shared my testimony before 180 men and women. Over twenty people gave their lives to God that night including tow homosexuals. God was using me. He was turning a bad situation into a good one, using me to glorify his name.

*"And we know that ALL things work together for good to them that love God, to them who are the called according to his purpose."*
-Romans 8:28

# 17
# God, Why Me?

Like many people, I asked the, "God, Why Me?" question. I looked back at my life, all the abuse, the crime, the hate, etc... I wanted to know what was so special about me. What did God see in me that I didn't see in myself. We never knew that we had already been chosen before all of the mishaps.

*"According as he hath chosen us in him before the foundations of the world, that we should be holy and without blame before him in love."*
*- Ephesians 1:4*

Satan had put the though in my head that I wasn't perfect enough for God. I wasn't good enough to work for God. I discovered that he wasn't perfect neither.

*"For all have sinned, and come short of the glory of God."* -Romans 3:23

Many of the people that God had chosen to work for him were sinners. As a matter of fact, all of them were, but some of the most notables were the following:

- Moses was a murderer. God used him to free his people from captivity and lead them through the wilderness and across the Red Sea. (Exodus)
- David was an adulterer and a conspirator. God used him to a king over Israel. (1 Samuel 16)
- Noah was a drunk. God used him to build an ark and to repopulate the world. (Genesis 6)

I used to and still to this day talk to different men that asked the same question. The conversation normally goes like this.
"Do you know how important your life is to God right now?"
"No!"
"Take the most famous dancing star to ever live, where is he now?"
"Dead."
"Where are you?"
"Still alive."
"Alright then. Evidently your life was more important to God than his was."

I heard about Carolina Panther's quarterback, Cam Newton's reaction after losing the Super bowl. I told him that God's sole purpose for creating his wasn't to win a Super bowl. I asked him what did he think was more important in God's eyes, him winning a Super bowl or all those kids' lives that he changed with a simple thing as giving away to them those touchdown celebration balls. That was his purpose. That was the gift that God gave him. God chose him to do that because he didn't bless every man with the same thing.

# 18
# The Acceptance

I had accepted God's purpose for my life, but Satan hadn't. He wasn't giving up so easily. He had flipped to the next page of his destroying book. He found another stick to throw at me.
"The white people did it!" That's what he had me thinking. After I forgave my mother, I wanted to know where she got the idea to have me killed for some insurance money. I done some studying and found out that Caucasian people were some of the first people to commit such and act. For a long time, people thought that I hated Caucasian, mostly Caucasian women, but I didn't. I hated their history and their ways.

Satan made sure that recognized any and everything when it came to a racial issue or something that involved a Caucasian woman and an Afro-American male. Especially the ones where the Afro-American men were being freed from prison as a result of being falsely accused of rape by a Caucasian woman.

I didn't hate Caucasian women. I was more afraid of them than anything. I remember when I worked in staff dining at the Grimes Unit. If a Caucasian woman came in there to get something to eat, I would fix her tray, then go stand outside the door until she left.

Satan pulled a trick. What did he do? He sent me to one of the units that's mostly known for its racist history. I was assigned to food service. I became the head cook after a couple of months. I was moved to another job on my day off. I had been falsely accused of being racist. I didn't lay down. I had the warden investigate the matter. I explained to him that I only talked about history. He wrote me back and told me that I was telling the truth and asked me what job did I want.

Days later, I was shipped to the Tucker Unit. A few weeks after I was there, God was tapping on my shoulder again. And I already knew why. "Son, I need you," "God, I don't want to go back to the RSVP program." "I need you to go over there and help those people." "I can't get through no yearlong program."

"You don't worry about that. Just go. I'll make something happen that you wouldn't believe." God told Habakkuk the same thing.

> *"Behold ye among the heathen, and regard, and wonder marvelously: for I will work a work in your days which ye will not believe, though it be told you."* -Habukkuk 1:5

I was being prepared. God was now answering a prayer that I prayed when I was in the Pal Program. It was the prayer of Jabez:

> *"God of Israel, Oh that though wouldest bless me indeed, and enlarge my coast, and that thine hand mith be with me and that thou wouldest keep me from evil, that thou wouldest keep me from evil, and that it may not grieve me."* -Chronicles 4:10

I now knew that I had been chosen and I knew why I had been chosen to do the will of God.

# 19
# Discovering My Gift

In 2008, I was incarcerated at the East Arkansas regional unit. That was the time when I fully recognized that I was gifted.

When you are "gifted", you are endowed with great natural ability, intelligence, or talent.
For years, society engraved in people minds that they had to go to college and receive a higher education if they wanted to make good money. But that has been proven not to be the truth.
The Library of Congress, United States Patent and Trademark Office can very well verify that people throughout history that discovered and created inventions didn't attend nor graduate college. Some never graduated high school. So, where did this gift, talent come from?

God gave the very first man a gift. Adam. He

gave him the gift to be a leader. He also gave Adam, Eve, as a help mate and companion as a gift. And he gave Adam and Eve the gift to reproduce and be fruitful.

All gifts were given to man by God. That's why they are natural. Man is naturally gifted.

*"Now there are diversities of gifts, but the same spirit. And there are differences of administrations, but the same Lord. And there are diversities of operations, but it is the same God which worketh all in all. But the manifestation of the spirit is given to every man to profit withal. For to one is given by the spirit the word of wisdom; to another to word of knowledge by the same spirit. To another faith by the same spirit; to another the gifts of healing by the same spirit. To another the working of miracles; to another prophecy; to another discerning of spirits; to the interpretation of tongues. But all these worketh that one and the self-same spirit, dividing to every man severally as he will."*
-Corinthians 12:4-11

God blessed us all with a different gift because we are one body and have many members, and all the members of that one body, being many, are one body; so also is the Christ.

Many people never discover their gift because

Satan has control of their mind. He never wanted me to discover the gift that God blessed me with because he knew that I would be using it to profit God's Kingdom and not his. This was God's purpose for man.

I am grateful for, not only God restoring my mental health, but for opening up my mind and showing me the gifts that he blessed me. It was always there ow that I think about it. When I was in school, the teacher would give us a homework assignment. I would do the assignment first. Then I would go to something else. One day, my teacher walked by my desk and she stopped. I was drawing a truck that had futuristic features. She looked at me as if she was thinking to herself, how did you draw that?

When I was a teenager, I built a set of wood steps so that my grandmother could get in and out the house. I had never studied carpentry before that. It's a gift from God.

Since God restored my mind, I have created the following:

1. 2- Board Games
2. 3 – Scratch off Lottery Tickets
3. 2 – Greeting Card Formats
4. 1 – Encrypted – Coded Computer Program
5. 1 – Baby Bottle Product

6. 1 – Floorplan For A 5- in-1 restaurant
7. 1 – Message In A Bottle by Mail
8. 1 – Newspaper Route GPS System
9. 1 – Stagecoach Limousine
10. 4 – Internet Websites
11. 1 – Multi-Task Elevation Ladder
12. 10 + Motion Picture Screenplays
13. 100 + song lyrics to include: R&B, Rap, Blues, Country, Rock, and Gospel

God blessed several men throughout the bible with different gifts:

- Noah with the gift to build (Genesis 6)
- Moses with the gift to lead (Book of Exodus)
- Joseph with the gift to interpret dreams (Genesis 40)
- Jonah with the gift to preach (See Book of Jonah)
- Jesus Christ with the gift to heal (See Book of Matthew, Mark, Luke, John)
- Martin Luther King with the gift to speak
- Whitney Houston with the gift of singing
- Walt Disney with the gift of creating Mickey Mouse
- Jim Carey with the gift to make people laugh
- Bob Baffert with the gift to train horses
- Chris Brown with the gift to dance

God blessed all these people with differences. They all have one thing in common. They profited from those gifts.

*"Some people misuse or never discover their gift because they did not retain God in their knowledge, God gave them over to a reprobate mind, to do those things which are not convenient: By Satan having control over their mind, people were and are filled with unrighteousness, fornication, wickedness, covetousness, maliciousness; full of envy, murder, debate, deceit, are malignity whisperers, backbiters, haters of God, spitefulness, proud boasters, inventors of evil things, disobedient to parents, without understanding, covenant breakers, without natural affection, implacable and unmerciful"*
- Romans 1:28-31

That's the very reason why we as children of God have to decide what we do with our gift.

# 20
# Spiritual Peace

I mailed the RSVP administrative Analyst a letter informing her that I was ready to participate in the program. I didn't know what the outcome was going to be. I only knew that I was going to give it my all.

I shared my testimony again at the Tucker Unit. On my way back to the barracks, I heard one guy telling another guy, "Man that's the most powerful testimony that I ever heard."

On Tuesday, October 6, 2015, I was transferred to the Ouachita River Correctional Unit to take RSVP. I made it to the unit and got comfortable. I asked my cellmate about the program. He explained to me that there was no more confrontation group (CG) and that class was only one time per day, four days a week. We could now listen to our music throughout the day. Stay in our cells as much as we wanted to. Once again, God had kept his promise. I believe that God will change anything, big or small, just for one man who's willing to do his will.

Satan wasn't done yet. I started writing grievances again. Staff didn't know what to do.

One day, I was in bed sleeping. I heard someone call my name. I got out of bed and went to see who it was. It was the captain. He told me to follow him that someone wanted to see me. We walked out in the hallway. There was the warden with a Caucasian woman. She told me that the RSVP staff wanted to help me, but didn't know how. She asked me what the problem was and I told her. She told me that I had to put the past behind me and move forward in life. I went back in the barracks then thought about who the woman was. I walked back out in the hub and asked the officer who the woman was. He informed me that it was the head director. I went back in my cell and laid down. I thought about what the woman said. God used her to tell me the same thing that the Apostle Paul told the Philippians.

*"Brethren, I count not myself to have apprehended: but this one thing I do, forgetting those things which are behind , and reaching forth unto those things which are before."*
-Philippians 4:13

I knew what was said, but something still wasn't right. I didn't participate in class. I stayed in my cell all the time. Something wasn't right. Satan only had one more thing to fight me with. What was it?

While I was in the Pal Program, I learned what the first part of the problem was, "Forgiveness." Even though my mother was the wrongdoer, I took the initiative to forgive her. I learned what prayer was. This being part two of the equation.

Forgiveness (Mark 11:25)
+Prayer (Matthew 5:44)

I struggled even though I forgave my mother. I was still missing something. What was I forgetting? Or who did I forget to forgive? Myself. People don't know this, but unforgiveness is the reason why they haven't received their blessings that they asked for. I knew the "problem" but not the "answer." Then I learned about who I was fighting. The inner me (enemy). I was in a "Me vs Me War." The Spirit Vs The Flesh. I kept fighting, telling myself that I was powerful and that I could complete the program and do whatever else that I wanted to do because,

*"I can do all things through Christ who*

*strengtheneth me."*                         -
                 -Philippians 4:13


    You see life is like a 3-part storm. You're either going into a storm, going through a storm, or coming out of a storm. This was a storm that I was going to come out of.

On January 1, 2016 at 12:01 am., I prayed to God and asked him to give e the answer to my problem. I went to sleep and when I woke up, he had given me the answer. I felt it in my soul.

Forgiveness (Mark 11:25)

+ Prayer (Matthew 5:44)

= Peace (John 14:17)

Jesus gave us peace. (John 14:27). Satan took it from us. (John 10:10). It's up to us to get it back. People asked me, "How did you overcome so much pain?"
"I had to press my way through."
The apostle Paul told the Romans:

*"In all these things we are more than conquerors through him who loved us."*
-Roman 8:37


I had gave up on God twice. I finally made a covenant with him and put on the whole amour of God.

*"Put on the whole Armour of God, that ye may be able to stand against the wiles of the devil. For we wrestle not against the flesh and blood, but of the darkness of this world, against spiritual wickedness in high places. Whenfore take unto you the whole Armour of God, that ye may be able to withstand in the evil day, and having done all, to stand."*                    -Ephesians 6:11-13

On January 8, 2016, the RSVP analyst, Ms. Donna Bost, other therapists and inmates sat quietly in the barracks as I shared my testimony with them. It's amazing how a woman that I disliked at first had faith in me when I needed the most. My own mother never had faith in me. But that's what God does. Sometimes you have to let God do God instead of you doing you.

The chaplain heard about my testimony. He asked me to share it with the unit and O.R.C.U. Pal Program.

On January 31, 2016, I'm doing as Jesus taught his disciples:

*"Let your light so shine before men, that they may see your good works and glorify your Father which is in heaven."*                    -
Matthew 5:16

I survived not one, not two, but three plots for me to die because:

*"No weapon formed against thee shall prosper."*
-Isiah 54:17

# 21
# A World Of Victims

I always wondered why, not only myself, but other people were not treated right by their family members and friends. Some of us were not treated right by strangers. There has to be a reason.

I used to wonder why did my mother do this? Or why did my father do that? I studied both my father's and mother's behaviors. I had some of theirs as well. My thought was – I learned my behavior from them. I've been predisposed to follow their example. That's why I have done the things that I have. That's what I thought. However, it's more than that. I only learned the extent of their influence over me was after I created a victim.

A "victim" is someone harmed by or made to suffer from an act, circumstance, agency, or condition. Or it can be someone who suffers injury, loss or death as a result of a voluntary undertaking.

I came to prison for having sex with an underage female. I created a victim even though she came to me. Why did I create a victim? Because I was a "victim of circumstance" at the time.

I hated my parents because I felt like they didn't teach me everything that I needed to know in life. I hated the school system because it didn't teach the whole truth. I hated everything until I took it upon myself to study history – Man's history. I studied man's history and discovered that history was only "his-story." There was only one history left for me to study - God's history. I did as the Apostle Paul told Timothy to do. (See 2 Timothy 2:15).

After a thorough research of God's history, I learned that we are living in "A World of Victims."

My parents created a victim (me). Your friend created a victim (you). The police created a victim (and unarmed innocent black male) because somewhere through life, someone created them as a victim.

"Victims" have been created since the beginning of time. The serpent created the first victim ever, Eve. (See Genesis 3:1-5). Eve created a victim – Adam. (See Genesis 3:6). Cain created a victim – Abel, his brother. (See Genesis 4:8)

Other examples of "Created Victims":

- Joseph by his brothers (See Genesis Chapter 37) -Envy & Jealousy
- Dinah by Shechem (See Genesis Chapter 34) -Sexual Abuse
- Uriah by David (See 2 Samuel Chapter 11) -Conspiracy
- Jesus Christ by The Romans (See Matthew Chapter 26 &27, Luke Ch. 22) – Non-believers
- Slaves by Slave Masters (See History Books and Movies)
- Students by Teachers (See the world we live in today)
- Children by Parents (See Prisons and Graveyards)

These are all examples of victims created by an act, circumstance, agency, or condition.

We all know that this is a major problem. I studied and learned the first part of the equation is "Disobedience." (see Genesis 3:14)

Since the "fall of man", men have chosen to disobey the commands of God. That's why Jonah ended up in the belly of the whole for three days. (See The Book of Jonah)

I learned that the second part of the equation is "Repentance." (See Luke 13:3). Victims continued to be created throughout generations because "no repentance." This resulted in them perishing.

Disobedience (See Genesis 3:14)
+Repentance (See Luke 13:3)

We would think that we have the problem solved, but we don't. I continued asking the question, why? I looked back at my life and asked myself this question. What was I missing? I was missing the "Knowledge of God." I discovered that this was the third part of the equation.

Disobedience (See Genesis 3:14)
Repentance (See Luke 13:3)
+Knowledge of God (See Hosea 4:6)
=A World of Victims

Victims are created because of these three things. If we know the "Knowledge of God", we will know the "Knowledge of Satan." Because God created the Good and Evil. We allow Satan to take advantage of us because we are ignorant of his devices. He knows exactly what to do and how to do it to you.

And this is how "he" creates victims. He uses "us." You see Satan is not in a physical human form like we are. He is a wicked spirit that we wrestle against. (See Ephesians 6:12)

So, in conclusion, we are living in a world of victims and have created victims because we lack the knowledge. That's why we have to forgive, forget, and love each other. We have to forgive our parents, friends, and our enemies, and even ourselves. Jesus did. (See Luke 23:34)

God bless you.


Sincerely,

A Living Testimony

Made in the USA
Columbia, SC
23 March 2021